Make A Killing On Kindle
Without Blogging, Facebook and Twitter.

The Guerilla Marketer's Guide To Selling Your Ebooks On Amazon.

By *Michael Alvear*

WOODPECKER**MEDIA**

ISBN: 978-0-9849161-5-3

Why You Need To Read This Book

Every day for three months I checked my Kindle sales and let out a string of cuss words that made my dog blush. They were beyond awful.

Then I developed the marketing strategies in this book and I opened my sales up like a soda can. Within three days I increased sales by a factor of ten. Within two months one of my books hit the #2 spot in its category, right below Chelsea Handler's latest release. And within three months I approached $10,000 a month in sales.

As word got out, authors flocked to me for advice, attracted to the methodical ways I turned guerilla marketing tactics into stellar revenue. One author client hired me to breathe life into an ebook that established a two-year residency in Kindle's basement. Its sales rank hovered around 550,000. In less than a week, I got it up to the 20,000 sales rank, hitting the Top 10 in two of her categories. These strategies work for me, they work for my clients, and they will work for you.

This book is for fiction and nonfiction writers overwhelmed by the complexity of selling on Kindle. It's for authors who won't leave a legacy publisher to strike out on their own without having a credible, go-forward marketing plan. It's for Kindle authors seething with frustration at their anemic sales. And it's also for the successful Kindle authors who want to take their success to the next level.

You have three obstacles that keep you from making a killing on Kindle:

1. **A Belief That You'll Be The Next Amanda Hocking.**
She's the Amazon superstar who got rejected by all the big publishers, threw her ebooks into Kindle with no marketing whatsoever, sold millions and ended up with a multi-million contract with St. Martin's Press. Admit it. You're secretly hoping you're next--that you'll put your book on Kindle and become an instant star, with money gushing at you like a broken fire main. Well, guess what? Lightning struck Amanda Hocking. It's doubtful it will strike you, even if you're a better writer. Don't let the fantasy make you complacent. Your book will succeed to the degree that you market it.

2. **A Belief That You Must Build An Author Platform.**
I know it's heresy to take an anti-platform stand, but I'm going to show you convincing evidence that the only people who can succeed are the already successful. You have to be a celebrity to have the kind of platform big enough to generate needle-moving sales. For example, that email list you're building? Only 30-34% of your subscribers will open it (that's the average "open rate" for email lists according to Constant Contact, the largest provider of email services). How many of the people who actually open your email will buy your book? About 1%, according to conversion

experts. I spent three years building an author platform of 30,000 follow-ers and it did almost nothing for my Kindle sales. Those are years I could have spent writing books and marketing them effectively. If you've got an author platform, stop building it. If you're thinking of starting one, don't. There are only two types of writers who should attempt it: Celebrities (because they've already got a built-in audience) and thought leaders who can use their platform to sell consulting services.

3. A Belief That Promotion, Publicity And Social Media Sell Books.
Three legacy publishers have published me. I've been interviewed on the top 30 radio stations across America, appeared on multiple talk shows including the Tyra Banks show, spent thousands on public relations, and countless hours building followers to my blogs and Facebook and Twitter accounts. It helped, but only in the way that rolling up the quarters in the back of the sofa helps pay the rent. You have got to get over the idea that you can sell books on Kindle through social media or outside promotion. It is a colossal waste of time. Book marketing is about getting the right book in front of the right person at the right time with the right copy and the right price. It is not about getting people to see your ad, read your blog post, click on your email or scan your tweet.

My book marketing strategy will take you 18 hours to implement. I know because I've timed it. How is this possible? Because there are only about a dozen things you can do on Kindle to truly make a difference in your sales. Everything else is a waste of time, including and especially, blogging, Twitter, Facebook and almost all of the old-school marketing and publicity tactics.

Before we get started I would like to make an appeal to you: Believe in your book. Nobody believed in mine and now I make a great living as an author. You can, too. In about 18 hours.

Introduction

My agent couldn't sell my last manuscript on dating, even though I had written three books under legacy publishers and starred in a reality show called The Sex Inspectors (it aired on HBO and in twelve other countries).

Then the recession hit and every magazine and website I wrote for died or went on life support. For ten years I had made a good living as a writer and then Bam! The floor went out from under me. For the first time I wrote for nobody. My career was over. Where would I go? What would I do?

I spiraled into a depression. Bills mounted. I lost my health insurance. I bounced around. I packaged my work into small ebooks and sold it off my blogs as downloadable PDF files. I generated some revenue but all it did was slow my descent.

I put three of these ebooks on Kindle. They tanked. I fell into a deeper depression. I had to borrow money from my parents. My humiliation was complete. But the money gave me just enough breathing room to reassess what I was doing. And one thing I noticed was that I bought into the Amanda Hocking fantasy that all you have to do to sell a book on Kindle is throw it up there with a decent cover and watch the money roll in.

 So I took a second look. I spent 20 years in the advertising, marketing and publicity industries before I became a writer, even winning one of the most coveted industry prizes-- Adweek's Media Plan Of The Year. If I couldn't figure out how to market on Kindle who could?

First, I pored over magazine profiles of Amazon superstars like Amanda Hocking to uncover the secrets to their success. It was as helpful as throwing a drowning man both ends of the rope. Most of the best selling Kindle authors who came out of nowhere to sell hundreds of thousands, even millions of ebooks, have absolutely no idea how it happened. Oh, sure, some will cite Facebook, Twitter and blogging, but I'm here to tell you that can't even begin to account for their success. Take Amanda Hocking. Right before her books took off she had about 500-1,000 visitors to her social media properties. Do the math. How can 1,000 people drive 2 million in sales? Not possible.

Then, I read every Kindle marketing book and article I could get my hands on. They were useless. Well, maybe not useless. *Anemic*. The recommendations were all things I already tried: Participating in forums, creating lists in Listmania, building email lists, sending out press releases and spending a lifetime toiling in the social media fields.

Let me be clear. You can sell more books by becoming active in forums or creating lists in Listmania. You can sell books with social media, eblasts, press releases and other tactics. But the payout is astoundingly low compared to the time you have to put into it. Do you have any idea how much time it takes to be a trusted member of a community forum, build a list, blog, tweet, Facebook, make videos, write reviews, distribute press releases, and send out email blasts? And for what? An incremental sale of 50, 100 even 200 books when you're looking for tens of thousands of sales?

As I pondered my discovery that profiles of breakout authors and Kindle marketing articles were of no help, I turned to a different approach. I completely immersed myself in Kindle, looking and interacting with it strictly from a marketing standpoint.

I soon realized that Kindle had its own ecosystem. And like any ecosystem, it is a world onto itself, immune to external factors outside its boundaries (like say, traditional marketing or social media).

To understand an ecosystem, a biologist has to know the climate, rainfall patterns, and other phenomena that nourish the soil to make things grow. To understand Kindle's ecosystem, you have to understand how one organism interacts with another. How do books compete and cooperate? And what goes on between books and readers that lead to a buy click?

You also have to understand the larger environment; that is, how the Internet influences the psychology of purchasing. And you need to learn the topography of one part of that environment—Amazon, and its main source of energy, the search engine.

Once I understood Kindle's ecosystem, I realized that marketing activity had to take place within its natural boundaries, not outside of them.

Fortunately, I was uniquely suited to develop strategies for this ecosystem. I not only had a 20-year career in advertising, marketing and promotion, I had in-depth experience in selling PDF-versions of ebooks from five blogs for over three years. This sharpened my expertise in SEO (search engine optimization) and "conversion selling," the process of engaging the customer in a way that leads to a buy click.

Certain dynamics must be in place for a conversion (a sale) to take place. So, when I see a tactic that violates, ignores, or diminishes those dynamics I know it's absolutely useless. I have tried every imaginable selling tactic. Some have led to spectacular failures, others to exquisite successes. And because of that, I have developed an exquisitely tuned bullshit detector for what works and what won't.

As I swam through Kindle's ecosystem I developed a three-word mantra: Attract. Engage. Convert. It's my shorthand for three bedrock principles:

1. Attract: You can't buy what you can't find.
2. Engage: You won't buy what you can't connect with.
3. Convert: You won't commit unless all your concerns are addressed.

Attract. Engage. Convert. These three words will help you navigate through Kindle's ecosystem, plant your books on rich soil and watch them grow as tall as redwoods. As I said before, when I first started on Kindle my ebooks were selling so badly they were re-enacting the death scene from Camille on a daily basis. I was selling a paltry one or two a week. But after unlocking Kindle's secrets and honing the Attract/Engage/Convert strategies I'm about to give you, each of those books zoomed into the Top 10 best sellers in their respective categories. And so did just about every book I've ever launched for my clients or myself.

One last thing before we get started. You must be a talented writer with a worthy book for a thirsty market or my strategies won't work. This book is not about the triumph of marketing over quality. It's about marketing quality. For the most part, the only thing marketing can do for a bad book is hasten its demise.

Assuming you fit the profile, let's get started. You're about to take an 18-hour journey to a potential best seller.

TABLE OF CONTENTS

ATTRACT. ENGAGE. CONVERT.
The Three Principles Of Kindle Marketing

ATTRACT: THE ART & SCIENCE OF GETTING BUYERS TO YOUR PAGE

Chapter Six
Did You Pick The Right Categories For Your Book?
- Amazon only lets you choose two. Strategies for picking the right ones.
- Increasing sales through "Category Leapfrogging."

Chapter Seven
Put A Billboard On Your Competitors' Pages.
- How to get people drawn to your competitors' book to buy yours.
- Using competitors as a sales trampoline.
- Five steps to getting into your competitors' "Customers Who Bought This Item Also Bought..." section.

ENGAGE: HOW TO GENERATE SERIOUS INTEREST IN YOUR BOOK

Chapter Eight
Writing 'Oceanfront' Book Descriptions.
- Nine reasons people won't buy your book and how to address them.
- A step-by-step guide to writing magnetic book descriptions.
- Examples of outstanding book descriptions: Fiction and nonfiction.

Chapter Nine
Revealed! The HTML Coding Secrets That Amazon Doesn't Want You To Know.
- Format your book description to look like a million bucks.
- Create different-sized headlines and fonts.
- Use bold, italicize, underline, center, and color formatting.
- Add pictures.

Chapter Ten
How To Use Amazon's "Look Inside!" Feature To Clinch The Sale.
- Customers can only see the first 10% of your book. Are you optimized for sampling?
- Eight ways to test if your "Look Inside!" sample will help or hurt the sale.

CONVERT: MAKING THE ACTUAL SALE

Chapter Eleven
Pricing Strategies.
- Why your goal should be revenue not price.
- The psychology of irresistible pricing.
- Five most effective launch prices.
- How to test post-launch prices.

Chapter Twelve
Getting Reviews That Make People Want To Buy Your Book.
- Yale University's study on the effect of user-generated Amazon reviews on sales.
- Placing "strategic starter reviews" that give browsers permission to buy.
- Getting good reviews by leveraging Kindle's 'Before You Go' feature.
- Why you shouldn't try to get all your friends and family to write a review.

Chapter Thirteen
Overcoming "Pre-Buyers Remorse"
- All unknown authors have a credibility gap. Bridge it with Author Central.
- Writing an effective author page.
- Examples of great author pages.

Chapter Fourteen
Is Your Book An Effective After-Sales Ambassador?
- Making the last few pages sell your other books & services.
- How to forge a strong personal connection with the reader.

Chapter Fifteen
How To Tell How Many Books You Sold By Looking At Your Sales Ranking.
- How many books will you sell if you achieve a 20,000 sales ranking? 2,000?
- How to use the relationship between sales ranking and units sold to forecast sales.
- Find out what your competition is earning.
- How does Amazon come up with their sales ranking?

Chapter Sixteen
Tying Everything Into One Glorious Knot.
Final thoughts, bits and bobs, and a plan to making sure you get everything done in 18 hours.

ATTRACT. ENGAGE. CONVERT.

Book marketing is about letting people know your book exists, impressing them with the content, providing "social proof" that they'll enjoy it, and removing every obstacle to purchasing it. I can sum up my marketing strategy in three words: Attract. Engage. Convert. You must learn how to overcome the unique obstacles in each of these phases of the book selling process if you want to add commas to your sales reports.

1. Attract.
You can't buy what you can't find and you won't buy what doesn't look good. Attracting book browsers to your page requires an artful mix of SEO (search engine optimization), standout covers, clickable titles and clever incentives. Attraction is a two-step process: Search And Seduce. First, you get to the top of Amazon's search engine results and then you seduce book browsers with the look, feel and content of your book.

Once, an international flight was forced to return to Paris by a misunderstanding. The air marshal on the plane discovered a handwritten message that said, "B-O-B". He interpreted it as, "Bomb On Board." But it turned out to be an acronym used by cabin crew to refer to an attractive passenger: "Best On Board."

Be a B-O-B.

2. Engage.
You've searched. You've seduced. How will you engage? Once you get them to your book page how will you create an emotional connection to your work? How will you phrase the "Book Description?" How can you merchandise the look of the page to make it more appealing? What will they see when they click on the "Look Inside!" button? How do you project relevance (nonfiction) or the promise of entertainment (fiction)?

All these questions go to content—the manuscript itself and the way you communicate its features and benefits. Your goal is to tell the truth but to tell it well.

3. Convert.

Have you removed all the obstacles to purchasing? Have you taken into account what stops people from clicking the buy button and addressed them? Many people could be primed to buy but your price puts them off (too high/too low), or they get nervous that nobody's reviewed the book. How do you overcome "pre-buyer's remorse?" That's the fear that you're about to buy something you'll later regret. It is a huge obstacle for first-time or unknown authors.

Attract. Engage. Convert. This is the model we'll be using going forward. Are you ready to rock? Let's roll.

CHAPTER ONE

The Myth Of The Author Platform And How It Stops You From Being Successful.

At its core, an "author platform" is the audience you've built for your book. It's the number of people that follow you in some way—through social media, speaking engagements, email lists, website traffic, articles, columns, etc. The premise behind an author platform seems to make a lot of sense: Build an audience and sell it books.

The industry has fallen in love with author platforms. Agents request it, publishers demand it, and writer conferences build seminars around it. What nobody tells you is that the only people who can do this successfully are the already successful. What nobody tells you is that unless you get hundreds of thousands of followers, your platform will sell a piddling amount of books. What nobody tells you is that the only way you can get that many followers is to become a celebrity.

Whoa, whoa, whoa. Hang on. Hundreds of thousands of followers? You need hundreds of thousands? I want to introduce you to a couple of concepts the platform peddlers never tell you about. The first is called a click-thru rate. That's the percent of people who click on an ad banner for your book. The second is called a conversion rate. That's the percent of "click-thrus" that convert to a sale. Now, what's this got to do with author platforms? Stay with me.

You can't sell your Kindle ebook directly from your social media properties. You have to re-direct people to Amazon via a clickable link. And that's where things get really ugly. Let's take your blog for example. There are two ways to send people to Kindle: Blog about your book or put an ad banner for it in a prominent position. The thing is, how many times can you blog about your book before you turn people off? Not many. So the ad banner has to do most of the heavy lifting.

Below you'll see a picture of how my sister does it. Note the prominent position of the ad for her book—in the upper right hand corner of her blog:

Nice, no? I'd say this is how 99% of writers with blogs promote their books. Well, I have some news that's going to shake you like a martini. Do you know what the average click-thru rate is for ad banners?

Three tenths of one percent.

That's not a typo. Three tenths of one percent. That's the industry average, according to *http://www.imediaconnections.com*, a digital marketing research service. To see their informative article on the subject click here:

http://www.imediaconnection.com/content/25781.asp

Now, think about what that means. Only three out of every 1,000 people who read your blog click on the ad banner for your book. Don't use up all your depression because there's more coming. See, you're assuming that everyone who clicks over will buy your book. Think again. About four percent of the three tenths of one percent of people who click on your ad will actually buy the book. How do I know? Experts from **InternetRetailer**, **PracticaleCommerce**, and **Emarketer** estimate that Amazon, the biggest, most recognizable name in ecommerce, runs about a 4% conversion rate.

Platform advocates always make it sound like people follow you so they can be sold to. So, if you have 10,000 people reading your blog that means you'll get nearly 10,000 book sales! But only a tiny fraction of that audience (three tenths of one percent) will click on the ad for your book and only 4% of that fraction will convert.

Let's do some math.

Let's say your blog generates 10,000 unique visitors a month (this would put you way over the average of most blogs and take you at least a year to achieve) and your blog has a big, prominent ad for your book the way my sister does. Here's how your sales would shake out:

10,000 Audience x .003 Click-thru = 30 Prospects x 4% Conversion = 1.2 Sales.

That's pathetic. Demoralizing. Depressing. A year of blogging and you end up selling one unit a month? Somebody pass me the Xanax. But wait, you say. Those numbers can't be right! My assumptions must be wrong! Well, click on the links above and check out the national averages for yourself—I didn't make them up. Let's say for the sake of argument that your book is so good that the click-thru and conversion rates are TEN TIMES better than the national average. Let's plug the numbers in:

10,000 Audience x .03 Click-thru = 300 Prospects x 40% Conversion = 120 Sales.

This is still pathetic. Assuming you can achieve click-thrus and conversion rates TEN TIMES higher than the national average you'll still only get one hundred twenty sales a month. That may sound like a lot to the newbie but it's a gonad-clinching number for writers who know they have to generate thousands of sales a month. Never mind the Xanax, somebody hand me the rat poison.

You need hundreds of thousands of followers to make an author platform work. If you're Nancy Nobody Or Nathan No Name, there is almost no way for you to build one with enough scale to generate significant book sales. By the way, when I use the word "significant" to describe sales, I don't mean dozens or hundreds of books here and there. I mean <u>thousands a month</u>. When I say "significant" what I really mean is career-changing. As in quit your job, pay your bills, fund your retirement and have a ball the rest of your life with income from your writing.

Don't get me wrong; there are lots of people who built enormous, profitable platforms. Bloggers like Darren Rowse of *www.problogger.net*, Seth Godin at *www.sethgodin.com*, and Jennifer Lawson at *www.theblogess.com* (all awesome sites, by the way) come to mind. But they didn't start with the intention of writing books. Rowse and Godin, for example, did it to generate income from advertising and market their consulting services. The books came later, and even then, they were initially PDF downloads. Bloggers like Lawson also make a lot of money through advertising and yes, they got book deals from traditional publishers, *but they were Internet celebrities by the time they got them.* Lawson's blog had nearly three million page views a month by the time she got her book deal. Platform peddlers point to Lawson's best selling book, *Let's Pretend This Never Happened* (Putnam) as a shining example of the power of a platform, but it's really an example of the power of celebrity. By the way, the sickeningly low click-through numbers and conversion rates I used earlier don't apply to celebrities, just to unknowns like you and me. The bigger the celebrity, the higher the rates for click-thrus and conversions.

Because it doesn't fit into their narrative, the platform peddlers omit a tiny detail: It takes years to build an audience large enough to propel real sales numbers. Years. Lawson started her blog in 2006. She got her book deal five years later in 2011. Do you have that kind of patience? Gandhi himself would reach for the brass knuckles the next time he heard somebody talk about the importance of platforms.

Don't Get Drunk On The Dream.
No discussion of author platforms would be complete without talking about everybody's favorite publishing dream, Amanda Hocking. She's the Amazon superstar who broke out of nowhere to get millions of sales and a multi-million dollar contract with St. Martin's Press. People assume that she became successful because of her platform. What platform? She had none. She's got one now, but that's because she became a celebrity. Don't listen to me; listen to her. Click below and read a long blog post she wrote about the secrets to her success. She doesn't even mention the word platform, even in the section where she advises struggling writers.

http://amandahocking.blogspot.com/2010/08/epic-tale-of-how-it-all-happened. HTML

Fiction Writers: You Have No Platform.
What in God's pajamas can you, as an unknown fiction writer, possibly blog, Facebook or Twitter about that would generate hundreds of thousands of followers? Yes, before she got popular, Amanda Hocking had a blog, a Facebook and a Twitter account. But she had a few hundred followers—almost all friends. She blogged about her life, not about her books. How on earth could it be any different? She writes about the supernatural—vampires, werewolves and the like. What could she possibly blog about that would attract a sizeable

audience? Characters in her books that at the time weren't selling?

Few fiction writers have the kind of subject matter expertise that translates into a big following. One exception might be historical fiction writers. For example, my sister specializes in Young Adult historical fiction. Her blog, *www. historywithatwist.blogspot.com*, is filled with entertaining bits of facts, theories and insights about antiquity. But even subject matter experts like my sister, who has four books to her name (the latest with Arthur A. Levine/Scholastic), generates maybe a few thousand visitors a month. She's been blogging for two years. Gandhi, where are those brass knuckles?!

Take it from somebody who teaches a class on blogging: There are great reasons to blog. Selling books isn't one of them. For example, my sister loves poking around the research and posting the nuggets she finds on her blog. She often uses these discoveries in her books. For example, she just discovered the ancient reason why we cover our mouths when we yawn (to keep demons from entering our souls). She's going to weave that into the book she's currently writing. She also loves the fact that thousands of people read her blog posts. If you have a driving need to blog about your field of expertise or about life in general, I highly recommend that you blog about it. Personal self-expression is an important part of a writer's life.

Just don't expect to sell many books.

My sister continues to blog, even though she knows it's done nothing for her book sales. Blogging has become an important way for her to stay connected to her research and express the love she has for history. This is as it should be.

Heresy 101: Stop Building Your Platform.

Build it and you will fail. Not because there's something wrong with having a loyal following (who wouldn't want that?) but because you could write five more books and market them effectively by the time you'd build an audience large enough to make a difference.

The people who insist an unknown writer must have an author platform to be successful have no idea how book marketing works. These well-meaning but wrong-minded platform peddlers insist that people will buy your book because the "platform" gives them a personal connection to you. Let me give it to you straight: Unless you're a celebrity, nobody is going to buy your book because of who you are. They're going to buy your book for what's in it.

Anatomy Of A Writer Who Got Sucker Punched By The Platform Peddlers.

Before I published my first ebooks on Kindle I listened to the platform peddlers and spent three years building my platform. As a sex and relationships expert, I built five dating blogs, three Facebook pages and two Twitter accounts. I had syndicated columns all over the country. I had YouTube channels. I co-starred in an international TV show that aired on HBO. I had thousands of subscribers to my email list. I think it's pretty safe to say that I had a bigger and better platform than most unknown authors. And yet my first ebooks on Kindle died on the vine. Three years of building my platform and all it gave me was a sales lift worth a few rolls of quarters. I cannot tell you how despondent this made me. I often drank a bottle of Jack Daniels alone, with a loaded gun on the table.

Why didn't my author platform work? Partly because it simply wasn't that big. Altogether, I'd say I had a total of 30,000 regular visitors to my social media properties. I believed the platform peddlers when they said people who follow you are interested in buying your books. They're not. They're interested in the free information, wisdom and entertainment that you provide.

But that's only part of the reason an author platform results in marginal sales. The bigger part is that your platform resides outside of the Kindle ecosystem, and as you will see in the rest of this book, almost nothing you do outside of Kindle will impact sales inside of it, unless you're a celebrity on the scale of Jennifer Lawson whose blog gets nearly three million page views a month. In the next chapter, I will explain in detail why the components of an author platform—blogging, social media, and email lists—violate almost every principle of effective book marketing. For now, I want to be your morality tale. I am what will happen to you if you go down the path of building an author platform. You will spend years, years, building an audience of a few thousand people when you need hundreds of thousands to have any impact. You will spend, as I did, thousands of dollars on tech support specialists, graphic designers, HTML coders, and email list services. You will spend, as I did, hundreds of hours learning things that have absolutely nothing to do with your field of expertise. You will spend, as I did, hundreds of hours giving away thousands of dollars in valuable writing for free.

Don't let me happen to you.

How Getting Rid Of My Author Platform Helped Me Sell A Career-Changing Number Of Books.

I was kidding about the loaded gun, but I drank my fair share of Jack Daniels. And during extended moments of sobriety I came to realize that I had to stop working on my author platform and come up with a better strategy. So I stopped blogging, I stopped sending out tweets, I stopped making videos and stopped trying to sell Kindle books with my email list. Instead, I concentrated on the things I could do within Kindle's ecosystem. And once I understood its dynamics I developed an effective system to catapult my ebooks to the top of their categories and start making career-changing money.

You are reading an expanded edition of Make A Killing On Kindle. It has been the #1 selling book on Kindle marketing for the last three months and ranks consistently in the Top 50 of all business books on Amazon. I have no author platform for this book. No blog, no webinars, no email list, no Facebook, no Twitter. Nothing. Zip. Nada. There were fourteen books on Kindle marketing by the time I published mine. Fourteen. Many of those authors had respectably large platforms and used social media to get the word out, yet my revenue is greater than all my competitors combined (see the chapter on sales/ranking to understand how I know). This is not an accident. They believed in the power of author platforms and social media. I believed in marketing within the Kindle ecosystem.

The Two Kinds Of Writers That Should Build Author Platforms.

There are only two kinds of writers that should attempt an author platform: Celebrities and subject matter experts (problem solvers, thought leaders, business authorities, spiritual leaders). They'd be fools not to build their own audiences. Not just because they've got one to begin with, but because they have the resources to hire people to do it for them. If you want to become a celebrity (good luck with that) then by all means, build your platform. If you are or want to become an expert, then you must build your platform, but not to sell books; to land consulting gigs. A top executive at Wiley Books, the biggest publisher of business books, courted an author friend and admitted that the average business book sells a mere 5,000 copies over the span of its life. Still, writing a book is well worth the effort for business authors because they offer the kind of credibility that helps sell $10,000+ consulting contracts.

Everyone else should work hard at getting platform amnesia, especially fiction writers. I'm sure there are examples that contradict what I'm saying but the bottom line is that you've been sold a bill of goods. Best selling books create an author platform, not the other way around. A ski instructor once gave me a piece of advice that I use in every area of my life: "Don't ski uphill." Point your skis the other way. It's a lot easier and a lot more fun.

Notes

CHAPTER TWO

Why Blogging, Facebook & Twitter Are A Complete Waste Of Time.

You can't swing a cat without hitting a Kindle marketing article that tells you to use social media to promote your books. Well, that cat needs to be put to sleep. There's one and only one situation in which blogging, Facebook, You-Tube, Twitter and other social media can sell books: If you're already a successful author with a bazillion followers.

Before I show you the convincing evidence that social media cannot sell an unknown author's book to save its life, I want to clarify a misconception. Despite what you hear, building a social media network isn't easy or fun. I run five blogs (for PDF ebook downloads) and four Twitter and Facebook accounts (for various non-book clients). I also teach blogging workshops. So when I tell you that social media is the most frustrating, time-consuming, energy-sucking, life-draining, stick-a-spoon-up-your-bum experience you can think of, I am saying it from a position of expertise.

First, you're going to experience so many technical problems you will contemplate one of two options: Murder or suicide. You will pay lots of money to strange people who tell you things you don't understand and don't want to know.

Blogs are particularly difficult to start and maintain. You don't get a lot of visitors by writing crap. Popular blogs feature well-researched, well-written posts. And that, as every writer knows, takes time. Lots of it. Time you are not getting paid for.

Don't be deluded into thinking it's easy to get followers to your blog, Facebook, Twitter, Tumblr, and YouTube accounts or to get people to subscribe to your email list. Let's take blogging for example. You have to know the principles of SEO (search engine optimization) and how to integrate them into the copy, headlines, title tags and architecture of the site or your audience will always be family and friends.

You also have to learn a fair amount of technology to operate your blog. You will have to learn basic HTML coding, how to search for, install and update plugins and widgets and how to back up the blog's database (or risk losing years of work). You will have to learn where to get royalty-free photographs and how to wrap text around them. It will take you a minimum of one to two hours to write an effective blog post and you'll have to do it at least three times a week to get on Google's radar. A lot of things will go wrong and after months of being held hostage to $60 an hour tech support specialists, you will develop Stockholm Syndrome. You will become a victim of learned helplessness. You will walk through your house in a catatonic state, thinking about your last will and testament as you practice tying knots.

Even small companies realize that getting critical mass on blogs and other social media takes full-time, dedicated employees to make it work. And those companies will be more than glad to tell you that it's almost impossible to sell through social media networks. They're wonderful to achieve communication and brand objectives, but sales? Not so much.

Let me give you an example that will put you off social media forever. I've been selling ebooks off my blogs for years now (they download as PDF files). After three years of intense work, the biggest blog in my portfolio attracts 25,000 unique visitors a month. That would be great if every one of those visitors were there to buy my books. But they aren't. They go to my blog to get information and be entertained. Do you know how many of those visitors actually go from my blog posts to the book page? About 5,000 a month. And that's only because I was smart enough to create a landing page with 3,000 words of ad copy. Let's do the math.

Unique Visitors to my blog	25,000 per month (after three years of hard work, mind you!)
Blog visitors clicking over to my book's landing page	5,000 per month (about 25% of all visitors to my blog)
Unit sales	50 per month (or 1% conversion)

Read it and weep. After three years of hard work I sell 50 PDF ebooks a month off my blog. That's less than two a day. But it would be even worse if, instead of selling PDFs, I sold my Kindle books. Why? *Because only 8-10% of the U.S. population owns a Kindle e-reader.* That means 90% of the people who go to my blog **DON'T OWN A KINDLE AND COULDN'T BUY MY BOOKS EVEN IF THEY WANTED TO.**

In other words, all those Kindle marketing books and articles are asking you to spend an eternity of blood, sweat and tears building a blog and getting Facebook and Twitter followers to attract people who don't own a Kindle e-reader. OMG!

Now, it's true that you don't need the e-reader to read Kindle books—you can just download the Kindle For PC/Mac application. But come on. How many people want to curl up with their desktop and read a good book? Before I bought an e-reader I downloaded the Kindle For Mac, thinking I could save money. It sucked. Yes, I saved money and yes, I could read the ebook I bought, but the user experience was worse than getting stuck in a conversation with a Kardashian. I bought the e-reader a week later. I suspect Kindle offers the PC/Mac download just so you can have a terrible enough experience to buy the Kindle Fire.

Which reminds me, don't do what I did when I published my first few ebooks on Kindle—save money by avoiding the expense of an e-reader. Huge mistake. It was only by immersing myself in the e-reader experience that I could truly understand how to sell in the Kindle ecosystem. If you are reading this book on anything but a Kindle e-reader, STOP. Buy one now.

But What About All Those Authors Who Got Book Deals From Their Blogs?

What about them? This book isn't about getting a book deal; it's about bypassing the gatekeepers, striking off on your own and selling thousands of books a month. But if you're still secretly hoping that a blog will attract an agent that will land you a book deal, you should know there are only two types of bloggers publishers look at: The type that have a massive following (in other words, celebrities like Jennifer Lawson), or the type that have a well-defined niche expertise. Take one of my blogging workshop alums, Christal Presley, as an example. She started a blog about her relationship with her father, a Vietnam veteran with PTSD. In addition to her own musings she developed an extensive resource for children of Vietnam War veterans. She got an agent and a book deal within a year of starting her blog, which at its height only got a few thousand followers. By focusing on a deeply personal subject—how to relate to a father with war-time PTSD—and creating an extensive resource that helped people like her, she became the kind of niche expert publishers love.

I don't discourage anybody from using a blog to showcase their writing. But selling a book deal is different than selling books. A blog can do the former but not the latter.

Do Email Lists Sell Books?

Yes. After two years of creating incentives to subscribe, managing and operating the email application system, and producing the kind of content that make subscribers want to open your emails, you will sell dozens of books a month! Yes, dozens!

Like all your marketing efforts, email list income has to be weighed against the effort it takes to generate it. Don't kid yourself—setting up and maintaining an email list is a difficult, time-consuming task. And there are costs involved. Most email services start at $30 a month and go up as your subscriber list grows.

Here's what you need to know about email lists: Nobody subscribes so they can be sold to. They're on it because you promised them information, wisdom or entertainment. If you don't produce consistently great content your subscribers will stop opening your eblasts. I don't know about you, but it takes me a long time to produce good content--time I could spend writing my next book.

As it is, industry "open rates" (the percent of people in subscriber lists who receive and open your emails) hover around 30-34%, according to Constant Contact, the largest provide of email services. *That means up to 70% of your subscribers don't open your emails!* Take it from somebody who's been there—it will take you years to build a list big enough to generate substantial sales. Years. Add to that the fact that only 10% of your readers will have a Kindle e-reader (okay, maybe 20-30% if they're big book buyers) and there you go again, getting sucked into a time-killing, no-value vortex of traditional marketing.

I'm not saying email lists aren't profitable. They are the golden goose for certain products and services. For example, the one I run for my blogging workshop is extremely profitable. Some people who sell their books in PDF download formats get stellar results from email lists. I have one for my PDF downloads and it does less than okay. In fact, I'm a pubic hair away from cancelling the email service. I've experimented with using my list to drive Kindle sales and the results were horrible, as I knew they would be. Selling Kindle books outside of Kindle violates a central principle of online selling: Do not EVER force people to leave your site to buy something. You'll confuse them and provide an opportunity to change their minds. This is compounded by the fact that 90% of your audience won't have a Kindle e-reader.

Don't Get Screwed By Social Media.

I'd like to share an interesting tale from a Sufi philosopher that helped guide me away from author platforms and social media:

> *A man was walking past the home of the Sufi rascal-sage Nasrudin one evening when he saw Nasrudin on his hands and knees searching for something under a streetlight. "Did you lose something?" asked the passerby.*

"My house keys," answered Nasrudin, distraught.

Being a good Samaritan, the man got down on his knees and began patting the grass along with Nasrudin.

A few minutes later another neighbor came by and joined in the search. Then another friend, and another, until a whole group of people were scouring the area.

After a long search, no one had any success. Finally someone asked Nasrudin, "Do you remember where you were standing when you dropped your keys?"

"Yes," answered Nasrudin. "I was standing over there," he explained, pointing to a darkened area quite far from where everyone was searching. "Then why are you looking over here?" asked one of his helpers.

"It was easier to look under the streetlight," answered Nasrudin.

Too many authors are bedazzled by the brightness of the social media street-lights when they should be looking in the darkened areas of the Kindle ecosystem. Forget about social media. It won't do squat to sell your book. I only recommend it AFTER your book hits it big. Then, it will be easy to get followers, Likes, Fans, and subscribers. But even then it will only serve as an effective sales tool for your next book. Not this one, the next one. Getting a lot of followers from your first book's success won't help with current sales because, well, think about it. Your first book produced all those followers! They're following you because they've already bought it and now they want what we all want when we follow somebody—free information, an entertaining experience or a few choice words of wisdom.

To review:

1. It will take you YEARS of incredibly hard work, a lot of money, and frequent urges to throw yourself off a bridge in order to get your social media properties to any kind of decent-sized audience.

2. The vast majority of the people who visit your social media properties or subscribe to your email list are not interested in your book. They're looking for free information and entertainment.

3. Ninety percent of your social media's audience won't own a Kindle e-reader.

4. Of the 10% who do, about 4% of them will "convert" to a sale.

Take it from somebody who teaches workshops on the subject: Social media gets you closer to sales the way jumping gets you closer to the sun.

Notes

CHAPTER THREE

Coming Up With A Must-Click Title For Your Book.

Developing an attention-getting title is perhaps the most challenging aspect of book marketing. Do not take it lightly as it will have a profound effect on sales.

The first thing you have to know about titles that sell on Kindle is something I teach in my blogging classes. I tell my students if they can grasp this one concept about the Internet they're destined for great things:

People don't read. They scan.

Simply put, if you're trying to reach me—the blog reader, or more specifically, the online book browser-- don't make me work to figure out the meaning of your title because I'm not going to take the time to do it.

The Internet is not a magazine, newspaper or book where you sit down for a good read and have the luxury of masticating every word. If you don't grab the reader quickly, they'll move on.

This argues for keeping titles short and instantly understandable. I should be able to read your title in less than five seconds and know exactly, without question, what your book is about. This is easier to do with nonfiction titles but you fiction folks should adhere to this principle as much as possible.

A Great Example Of What Not To Do.

I had a client come to me because her book on infertility was selling so badly she could practically hear Amazon laughing at her. I thought she was going to have a stroke when I recommended she change the title of her book. She was very upset. She had actually trademarked the title, and used it everywhere in her marketing materials (she's an infertility therapist). Thankfully, she relented.

This was her title:

Hopeful Heart, Peaceful Mind
Managing Infertility

Quick! Tell me what this book is about. You can't. Not really. Yes, of course, it's about infertility, but how vague is that? Is it about the latest infertility treatments? About managing your infertility doctor? The title has a kind of Zen feel to it. Is it about meditations to enhance fertility? It's anybody's guess.

This brings us to my fundamental premise about titling books:

DO NOT LEAVE ROOM FOR INTERPRETATION.

If I can't tell what the book's about in the title there is very little chance I'm going to click on it to find out. I have better things to do. Remember, I don't read; I scan. And if I scan a book title that doesn't tell me exactly what's in the book I'm on to the next one.

Here is the new title I developed:

Managing The Stress Of Infertility
How To Balance Your Emotions, Get The Support You Need, And Deal With Painful Social Situations When You're Trying To Get Pregnant

Is there any doubt about the content of this book or whom it's for? Notice two things: It has a short title and a long subtitle. While this is admittedly almost impossible to do with fiction, it's something highly advisable for nonfiction. The short title tells you what it's about while the long title explains the benefits.

Did my client's new title work? It bears repeating that her book languished in Kindle's basement for two years, selling an average of one or two books a month. When we re-packaged it with the new title (and all the marketing strategies in this book) it hit the Top 10 Books On Infertility within two weeks. Same book, same price, different marketing strategies, stellar results.

If you already have a title for your book you might want to consider changing it, even if it's already up on Kindle and requires you to create a new cover. It will make a huge difference in your sales.

How To Come Up With Great Titles.

As you'll see in a moment, there are many ways to get a powerful book title, but if you want the fastest method, look in your manuscript. The perfect title for your book is most likely a line or phrase buried deep within it.

I remember showing the manuscript of my first book to my sister (she's also a writer—check out why Publisher's Weekly gave her book on *Cleopatra's Daughter* a starred review). I was at her door about to leave when she said, "Oh, one last thing. You need a better title. It's right here on page 25 (pointing to a line I had written)—" Men Are Pigs But We Love Bacon."

I gave the same advice to a fellow writer, Hollis Gillespie. She had a crappy title for her book. I scanned her manuscript and said, "Here! Here's your title: Bleachy Haired Honky Bitch. She actually ended up on the Tonight Show, in part, because the producers loved the title so much.

Bottom line: Let your book title itself. Go through your manuscript. It's in there somewhere.

Of course, many times the perfect title isn't in your manuscript. That's why you need to learn...

How To Brainstorm Your Book Title.

There is no single way of arriving at a great moniker. But if you use some combination of the following brainstorming techniques, the road to that magnificent title will be short and paved with precious metals.

Brainstorming Tip #1.
- Write down a single paragraph that best describes your book.
- Write down all the verbs you used in the above paragraph.
- Write down all the nouns you used in the above paragraph.
- Write down all the combinations of nouns and verbs you used above to form titles.

Don't worry if these combos don't click at first. This is a process. Even great authors come up with nose-pinching drafts. Do you know how F. Scott Fitzgerald originally titled *The Great Gatsby*? Trimalchio In West Egg.

Brainstorming Tip #2.
Go to Amazon or your local bookstore (I know, what's that?) and browse through your genre. Write down twenty titles that you like. Ask yourself these questions:

- Why does this title work?
- What do I like about this title?

- What don't I like about this title?

Now, sit down with a pencil and paper (I know, what's that?) and blend your book into some of the titles you love best. Let's say you are writing a book about your disillusionment with Eastern meditative practices, and one of the titles on your favorites list is *Eat, Pray, Love.* You could easily insert your book into this title by naming it, *Eat, Pray, Hurl.* The point isn't to be a copycat; it's to generate ideas that lead to other ideas.

Brainstorming Tip #3.
Write down every attribute of your book and then "free associate" these characteristics with something concrete. Here's a great example of free-associating. In a brainstorming meeting, a super glue company asked, "What are the glue's attributes?" Someone said, "It's strong." The moderator then asked, "What comes to mind when you say 'strong'?" Someone blurted out, "Gorillas!" They ended up naming their product Gorilla Glue.

Brainstorming Tip #4 (Fiction Only).
- Write down words that describe or suggest the setting.
- Write down your major characters and words that relate to them.
- Write down verbs that capture what you want readers to think or feel.

Now, from these lists come up with about 10-15 titles. Pretend your subconscious mind is a preheated oven. Now put those titles in a baking sheet, lower the temperature and check back in a day or two to see which ones rose.

Brainstorm Tip #5.
Write down the subject matter of your book and change a letter or word to alter its meaning.

Example #1: The Dalai Lama --or his work-- is a subtheme of your book.
1. Write down the subject matter: Dalai Lama.
2. Start changing letters or words. Like: Dalai Mama.

Example #2: Your book is about the art of debating effectively.
1. Subject matter: verbal kung fu.
2. Change letters or words: Tongue Fu.

Brainstorm Tip #6.
Draw a vertical line down a sheet of paper. On the left, write down the logical aspects of your book. On the right, the emotional, creative and aspirational. Now, combine words from each column. Example: Catch-22.

Brainstorm Tip #7.
Take a cliché or saying and start replacing words or letters. Say you've got a cooking book. For some reason you like the saying, "Beauty And The Beast."

Change a letter and you've got Beauty And The Yeast. Other examples:

"Life is a Cabernet."
"I think therefore IBM."

Some very popular books are based on clichés:

Midnight Sun.
City Of Fallen Angels.
Two-Way Street.

Start by identifying a key word and then look up how it's used in a cliché by going to one of these sites:

http://www.westegg.com/cliche
http://www.clichesite.com
http://clicheweb.cambiaresearch.com/clicheweb/

For rhymes, you can't beat these sites:

http://www.rhymezone.com/
http://www.rhymer.com/
http://wikirhymer.com/

Where To Look For Book Title Ideas.

Good ideas are orphans. They don't know who their parents are. Your job is to look for those urchins in places you may not have thought of. For example:

Jokes, Anecdotes And Stories.
Take the title of the best seller Eats, Shoots and Leaves. Author Lynne Truss said it came from a joke that illustrates the dangers of one misplaced comma:

A panda walks into a cafe, orders a sandwich, eats it, then draws a gun and fires two shots into the air.

"Why?" the waiter asks.

The panda shows the waiter a badly punctuated wildlife manual. "I'm a Panda," he says. "Look it up."

The waiter finds the relevant entry: "Panda. Large black and white bear-like mammal, native to China. Eats, shoots and leaves."

Song Titles Or Lyrics.
Some of the best titles for anything can be found in songs. Here are just a

few examples:

Hazy Shade Of Winter
Moondance
The Devil Went Down To Georgia
Lady In Red
Truly Madly Deeply

To get more song ideas click over to www.billboard.com. They've got every list imaginable: Top 100 songs in country, rock, pop, etc.

The Six Types Of Book Titles.

1. Shock Titles.
These are attention-getting phrases that surprise because they either go against conventional wisdom or they're so vivid in and of themselves. Examples:

Another Bullshit Night In Suck City.
Why Men Marry Bitches.
I Hope They Serve Beer In Hell.

2. Story/Metaphor Titles.
These are titles that revolve around an anecdote or observations. Examples:
Chicken Soup For The Soul.
Eat That Frog.
Ready, Fire, Aim!

3. Contrarian Titles.
The best ones challenge our assumptions and threaten the status quo. Examples:
Hitler's Jewish Soldiers.
Eat Chocolate, Drink Alcohol And Still Be Lean And Healthy.
How To Lose Friends And Alienate People.

4. One-Word Titles.
Beloved.
It.
Influence.

5. Long Titles.

Nonfiction:
How To Get Rich Working Two Days A Week.
How To Win Friends And Influence People.
Men Are From Mars, Women Are From Venus.

Fiction:
The Curious Incident Of The Dog In The Night-Time.
Fried Green Tomatoes At The Whistlestop Café.
Wicked: The Life & Times Of The Wicked Witch Of The West.

6. Dialogue Titles.
The classic example of a book title with a dialogue line:
He's Just Not That Into You.

Pay attention to conversations—yours or the ones you have no business eavesdropping in on. Keep an ear out for conversations in movies, TV or your favorite morning DJ. If it's a nonfiction book, listen to your clients. What do they say a lot? What turns of phrase do they use?

All About Alliteration.
The Oxford American Dictionary defines alliteration as, "The occurrence of the same letter or sound at the beginning of adjacent or closely connected words." It's their fancy way of saying beat and cadence. The best book titles almost always have some form of alliteration:

It's Not What You Sell, It's What You Stand For.
Something Wicked This Way Comes.
To Kill A Mockingbird.

Testing Your Book Title.
Narrow your field to three possible titles and test them against these questions:

- Does the tone of the title match the tone of the book?
- Does it convey the right genre? The right time period?
- Would it attract attention if it were on a bookshelf and you could only see the title?
- Does the title leave any room for interpretation? (Applies more to nonfiction)

It's important that you get feedback for the titles you come up. You will eventually be "The Decider," but until that moment you should be getting input from people you trust. Once you've winnowed down the field to three titles, try this process:

Establish an advisory council of "book murderers." They should be writers, editors or people in marketing or PR who have a history of killing your ideas with their bare hands. In other words, don't ask your mom (unless your mom's really mean). Your council should be made up of 6-8 people so that you can get a range of opinions. It's important to only seek advice from your advisory council. Do not to fall into advice-seeking promiscuity. You will end up with things it will take a clinic to get rid of.

Call three of the most trusted people in your advisory council and read the titles out loud. Do not email it to them. They're likely to read the titles, stew on them and give you a thoughtful answer. You don't want that. You want reactions not opinions. Remember what I said earlier about the Internet: People don't read; they scan. A drive-by impression will be far more useful than a thoughtful critique.

Here's how it should play out on the phone. You call your trusted confidant. You say the title out loud. What did they do? Pause? (bad). Laugh? (good). Stutter? (bad) Exclaim? (good). What is the tone in their voice? Confused, apathetic, excited? I have never been talked into a title, but I've been gut checked into one plenty of times.

Email the best titles to the rest of your advisory council. After you make a few phone calls and get input, you'll probably make some changes to the title. Now it's time to email your full council.

Do not ask your advisory council to come up with ideas. First, that's an imposition for most people because it takes so much time. Second, they don't know the criteria for your book title so you're likely to get off-the-mark suggestions. Instead, ask them to rate the titles you developed.

Take their ideas and make adjustments accordingly. Some people will simply tell you what they like, others will tell you what they don't and how to fix it.

Be the decider. Once you've gotten all the input, it's time to decide. This is easy to do if there's a clear-cut winner, but often there's not. In that case, go with your gut. And just to relieve the pressure a bit, the great thing about Kindle is that if you feel the title ends up working against you, you can always change it.

CHAPTER FOUR

Designing A Book Cover That Ignites Click Lust.

"If you have already passed that hurdle of having a customer be attracted to the cover, and then they pick up the book," said Patricia Bostelman, vice president for marketing at Barnes & Noble, "an enormous battle has been won."

--New York Times

When have you ever bought a book with an awful cover from an author you've never heard of? I know I haven't. If a good title is a magnet to book buyers, a good cover is the superconducting particle accelerator. It collides books with buyers. In seconds, you attract a reader's attention away from the competition. It buys you first impressions and second chances. Covers form instant opinions in a single snapshot. They have the power to shape the perception of the story and the strength of your writing. In the mind of a book buyer, covers mean quality. The better the cover, the higher the quality.

So let me get straight to the point: Never, EVER design your own book cover. I don't care how good you think you are, you're going to end up with something so ugly it'd make a train take a dirt road.

Of course, hiring a designer costs money, but you should see it as the single best financial investment you can make in your book. Depending on the complexity of the cover and the depth of the designer's experience it can cost as little as three hundred dollars to as high as a couple of thousand.

Let's talk about budget for a second because I know even $300-$500 can be an obstacle for a lot of writers. You bought my book because you want to make a living off of Kindle. Well, just like you can't make the dough rise in the oven without turning on the heat, you can't make it rise in Kindle without opening your wallet.

A cover that costs $300 may be a lot of money for a struggling writer, but if it helps you generate even a measly $1,000 a month ($12,000 a year), that "cost" sounds more like an investment to me. If you could turn $300 into a $12,000 annuity, you'd be a fool not to beg, borrow, or steal the money.

How To Choose A Book Designer.

High-end.
You want a professional book designer like Carl Graves, who does a lot of work for best selling authors like J.A. Konrath and Barry Eisler. You can find him at *http://extendedimagery.blogspot.com.* Of course, he's not the only one—there are many, but their cost goes into the high hundreds or low thousands depending on what you need. How to find them? Look for covers you love from Kindle-only books. It's a mark of an indie author who isn't backed by legacy publisher. Meaning, they hired a freelance book cover designer they'd be happy to refer to you. Follow the author's blogs (if they have one) to see how to contact them.

Middle-End.
The best way to find experienced book designers in a more affordable category is to go through one of your local book printing companies. They hire dependable graphic designers who work on a ton of self-published books. You can also get referrals from other self-published authors in forums or blogs like *http://www.selfpublishedauthors.com.*

Low-End.
It's always best to choose a seasoned, professional book designer but any capable graphic designer can do the job. For affordable but experienced designers (try to get somebody with three to five years of design experience) do a search on *www.guru.com* or *www.elance.com.* For the absolute cheapest alternative, go to *http://99designs.com.* You set a price you're willing to pay and they set up a contest among the designers willing to work on your project (the higher the price, the more likely you'll get a lot of designers). This is a great way to get multiple book covers to choose from. There are some truly amateur designers on this site, so buyer beware.

How To Manage Your Graphic Designer.

I've managed graphic designers at several ad agencies over the years. There's a right way and a wrong way to get good work from them. Here are the golden rules:

Tell them what you want, not what to do.
Telling a graphic designer to use this color, that graphic or this font is a great way to get a bad result. You don't want them to simply regurgitate your preconceived ideas. You want to access their creativity. Manage the process; don't micro-manage the results.

Give them parameters.
If necessity is the mother of invention, constraint is the father of creativity. Designers like a certain amount of constraint in their work because it gives them something to push against. There are two worst-case scenarios for a

designer: The client who says, "Do whatever you want" and the client who hands them a list and says, "*I want everything in it.*"

There's as much danger in giving a designer too much information as there is in not giving him or her enough. Suppose The New York Times came to you and said they wanted an article from you on anything you wanted to write. You'd flounder. But if they said, "We want an article on pro athletes who started out as ballet dancers," you'd have something you could sink your teeth into.

Tell them size matters.
The main parameter for your designer is simple: The cover has to pop as a postage stamp. Kindle covers make printed book covers look like a well-endowed lover. They are so small they make you weep and reach for the male enhancement pills. If it can't pack a punch as a postage stamp, your Kindle dreams will turn into nightmares. It's important to realize that your book cover is going to appear in three areas:

The Kindle e-reader or Kindle reading app for your PC. Your cover will appear in thumbnail size and mostly in black and white (only the newest Kindle e-readers offer full color).

Your book's landing page. Seen through your pc's browser, it's about the size of two postage stamps and always in full color.

Various Amazon.com areas (as seen through your computer's browser). This includes search results and the "Customers Who Bought This Item Also Bought..." Again the sizes range from one to three postage stamps.

Ground Rules For The Unendowed Cover.
1. Subtlety doesn't work. What works for an 8" x 5.4" trade paperback book cover jacket is not necessarily going to work for a 7/8" x 1" Kindle cover.
2. Make sure the title can be read CLEARLY. Sacrifice the readability of the subtitle if you must. It's better to get the gist of the book clearly, than to squint and fuss, trying to understand what the hell any of it says.
3. Use images that are crisply delineated.
4. Use bold fonts.

Getting The Best Out Of Your Graphic Designer.
Send them what's known as a creative brief (a single page document that details what you're looking for) and then have a brainstorming session. Here is an example of a creative brief I sent to my designer:

Creative Brief For Flirty Text Message Helper Cover Design.

Title: The Flirty Text Message Helper.

Subtitle: Witty Texts For Clever People.

What the book's about: A collection of funny, flirty, texts you can send to impress the guy or girl you're crushing on. It's classified by 19 dating "situations," like getting a girl's number who doesn't seem all that interested. Or getting the number of a girl that's just as interested as you are. Example:

You: Stop.

Likely Reply: Stop what?

You: Stop thinking about me. See, you're doing it right now. STOP.

Target demographic: Men and women 21-35.

The promise of the book: Build the kind of attraction that leads to a date, a hookup, or the beginnings of a great relationship. It's also a jump-start for your own creativity. Sometimes you get so nervous when you meet somebody you like your brain freezes and you don't know what to text.

What emotion I want the book browser to feel when they see the cover: A sense of fun, whacky excitement. I want to remind them how much fun it is to send or receive a text from someone they're interested in.

Specs:
- Must be noticeable at postage stamp size.
- Use bold fonts that make the headline instantly readable.
- Use simple images.
- Bold, primary colors preferred.

The creative brief doesn't have to be any more complicated than simply telling the designer about the book, your preferences, and what you want the reader to experience. You want it in writing though. Yours isn't the only project they're working on—they need something to refer back to.

Your graphic designer should deliver three different concepts. You can determine which one to go with by asking these questions:

- Is the title legible at such a small scale?
- Does the image tell a story?
- Does the design echo the book's tone, theme or mood?
- Would I want to know more about this book based on a five second glance?

Be Demanding And Don't Settle For Good Enough.

A Jewish grandmother and her grandson are at the beach. He's playing in the water while she's standing on the shore not wanting to get her feet wet, when all of a sudden a huge wave appears from nowhere and crashes directly onto the spot where the boy is wading. The water recedes and the boy is no longer there. He was swept away.

The grandmother holds her hands to the sky, screams and cries: "Lord, how could you? Haven't I been a wonderful grandmother? Haven't I been a wonderful mother? Haven't I kept a kosher home? Haven't I given to the B'nai B'rith? Haven't I lit candles every Friday night? Haven't I tried my very best to live a life that you would be proud of?"

A voice booms from the sky: "All right already!"

A few minutes later another huge wave appears out of nowhere and crashes on the beach. As the water recedes, the boy is standing there. He is smiling and splashing around as if nothing had ever happened.

The voice booms again. "I have returned your grandson. Are you satisfied?"

The grandmother says, "He had a hat."

Don't settle. Be demanding. The cover of your book is too important. I use a fantastic designer for all my books. Usually, he gives me three concepts and I choose one. But for the cover of this book, he must have done 12 concepts because I wasn't feeling the love for any of them. Our relationship got strained and we even talked about parting ways. I knew the issue wasn't his talent but the challenge: How do you communicate the promise of making money without lapsing into tired visual cliches? Almost all my competitors used pictures of money on their covers. I had to stand out, but how? How could I get better work out of my designer? By being communicative and collaborative, but mostly by being demanding. By not settling. By not being afraid to say, "He had a hat."

Notes

CHAPTER FIVE

How To Get To The Top Of Amazon's Search Engine Results.

There are five ways a book buyer can find you:

1. *Keyword Search Results.*
Putting a search term in Amazon's box ("books on infertility," "Cleopatra," "Vampires").

2. *An Association With A Competitor.*
Appearing in a competitor's "Customers Who Bought This Item Also Bought..." section.

3. *Category Listings.*
Clicking on the category link of a competitive book, which takes them to the "Best Sellers" list in that category. The higher you rank, the easier it is to find your book.

4. *Browsing Through Kindle's Lists.*
This includes sections like Book Deals, Best Sellers, etc.

5. *Direct Search Results.*
Typing your name or the name of your book in Amazon's search engine.

> * There are other, smaller ways, like creating lists in Listmania, participating in forums, getting interviewed by outside bloggers, seeing a tweet or a Facebook post, etc. but they represent marginal sales at best. Remember, we're aiming for career-changing sales.

Why your best hope is to rank high on Amazon's search engine. Outside of being a celebrity or already being in the top 20 in your respective category, your only hope for serious coin is to show up in Amazon's search results whenever somebody looks for a book in your category. To bring this point home, let's look at a scenario:

1. Potential customers are looking for a book like yours. They type in keyword phrases into Amazon's search box.

2. Amazon's search spiders shoot out through the site and look for these phrases. They don't see them in your book's title, book description or search profile (the 7 keyword phrases Amazon allows you to submit to their search engine).

3. Your book doesn't show up in the search results. Or it shows up on page 40.

4. No sale.

Don't let this happen to you. Unless you're a celebrity, an author with a sizable fan base, or have a book that is already selling well, customers are not going to find you unless you rank high in their Amazon search results.

Wait. I fear I have understated the case, so let me put it more bluntly:

YOU ARE DESTINED TO FAIL IF YOU DON'T USE THE RIGHT KEYWORDS.

Your goal is to land in the first page of Amazon's search results. For comparison purposes you probably know that Google lists about 10 search results per page. Amazon lists about 20. On Google, about 80% of people stop searching after page 3. I suspect it's probably the same on Amazon.

Here's my definition of a keyword phrase: The words buyers plug into Amazon's search box when they're looking for a book like yours. Your job is to find out what those words are, for they are your paths to glory. You'll find out how to do that in a moment. For now, I want you to see that there are three places you can embed these all-important keywords:

1. The title of your book.
2. The "Book description" in your book's landing page.
3. Your book's search engine profile (Amazon allows you to define your book in seven keyword phrases).

Discovering What Keyword Phrases People Use To Find Your Type Of Book.

Again, a keyword phrase is basically a word or series of words that browsers put in Amazon's search box to find a book. Since a great deal of people who buy books don't know which book they want to buy, they punch in phrases that help them narrow the field.

Unfortunately, Amazon provides zero information on the type of keyword phrases you should use. Fortunately, there are ways to back into the information:

1. Use Google's Adwords Keyword Tool To Get A List Of Keyword Phrases.

Google will tell you the exact phrases people plug into its search box when they're looking for information contained in your book. This is the first step toward developing the keyword phrases you'll use in your Kindle account.

Let's take the example of my ebook, The Flirty Text Message Helper: Witty Texts For Clever People. I'm trying to reach guys and girls who want ideas on what to text their crush. I don't know exactly what these people are typing into Google's search box, but I can start with a few guesses. So I go to www.google.com/AdWords and type in:

"Flirty text messages"
"Flirt text"
"What to text a girl"

Flirty text messages:	14,800
Flirt text:	60,500
What to text a girl:	201,000

According to Google, here are the number of monthly searches for each of the keyword phrases I asked about;

Love text messages:	165,000
How to text flirt:	60,500
What to text a guy:	92,500

Google also gave me a list of hundreds of other keyword phrases I might want to use. Here are a few:

So, I make a list of the keyword phrases I think are most helpful and relevant to me and move on. Once you understand how people are searching for the informational content of your book on Google, you can use that information (with the "Leading Indicators" I'll show you in a minute) to determine your keyword phrases on Amazon.

Ah, you say, that's all fine and good if you're writing nonfiction. But what about my paranormal book on werewolves? Or my historical novel about Van Gogh? How can I use this strategy for fiction titles?

Let's take the werewolf book as an example. You do a keyword search on werewolves (https://adwords.google.com/) and Google tells you there's an astounding number of information seekers:
Keyword Phrase: Werewolf
# of monthly searches: 673,000

And what kinds of questions are over half a million werewolf fanatics asking? Here's a sampling from Google...

"How to kill a werewolf"

"What do werewolves eat?"

"What's a lycanthrope?"

If I had a book that featured werewolves, I'd get busy finding keyword phrases they use on Google. In some ways, Google keyword search has more potential in fiction than in how-to. Why? Because fiction writers delve into multiple subject matters in a single book.

Let's pretend your book is a whodunit set in Barcelona's Barri Gotic area (Gothic Quarter). The setting alone, along with the history of the city, draws about 10,000 Google searches per month. Let's say you write in great detail about police procedures like fingerprinting (550,000 Google searches per month), and your heroine lives in a building designed by Gaudi, the Catalon modernist (90,500 Google searches per month). Shall I go on?

Passion powers the information seeker. There is no subject that you can write about that doesn't have thousands, hundreds of thousands or millions of fanatics trying to satisfy their fascination through Google searches. Once you compile a list of about 20 keyword phrases from Google, it's time to...

2. Use Amazon's Secret "Leading Indicators" To Rank High In The Search Results.
I want you to try something right now. Go to Amazon's search box and type in "How to." You'll see a drop down menu of popular Amazon search terms that start with "How to." Now type "how to text" and you'll see another drop down menu. Notice the "how to text a guy" and "how to text a girl?" phrases in the drop down menu? Amazon is auto-filling the search box with words that people use to find books like my Flirty Text Message Helper. Bingo!

Notice, if you will, how the phrases in the drop down menu are organized. They're not alphabetical. Since Amazon doesn't do anything without a precise purpose, we can use Sherlock Holmsian logic to deduce that they're ordered by popularity.

Now, how popular are the keyword phrases in the drop down menu? Nobody knows and Amazon ain't saying. But there's gold in them thar hills because they are "Leading Indicators" of what Kindle browsers are looking for. Think it only works for nonfiction books? Watch. Type in "vampires" and look at the drop-down. Click on any of them and see what comes up—books that are optimized for that search word. Magic!

Now here's where the art comes in: Unlike Google, Amazon doesn't tell you how many people searched for the keyword phrase you typed in. It could be ten; it could be ten million. That's why I call them Leading INDICATORS, not Leading Facts. So you have to rely on what makes the most sense to you. Follow your gut. Just because a keyword phrase shows up in Amazon's drop-down menu when you type it in the search box doesn't mean a ton of people are using that phrase. Also, be careful about what you type in because once you type in a full keyword phrase Amazon remembers it. The next time you log on and dig for Leading Indicators, it will spit out that keyword phrase as if other people typed it in. Avoid this pitfall by conducting your Leading Indicator research in one session.

Even though you can't substantiate how popular a Leading Indicator is on Amazon, a clue is a clue. And if that's all you have to go on, then you go with it. There are no formulas, but there is one guiding question:

What keywords best describe the content of my book?

In my example, the keyword "Flirting" is wildly popular. So is "texting." But these two words have varying contexts that have nothing to do with my book. For example, "How to flirt" doesn't do me any good because, in my opinion, most people searching under that phrase are looking for face-to-face flirting techniques. "Texting" has a similar problem. A lot of the searches for that word are from people looking for information on how to text through the Kindle e-reader or the best free texting services. Ahh, but let's put those two words together ("flirt texting") and Bingo! THAT'S a relevant keyword phrase for me.

I can't stress this enough—there is no replacing your own judgment. At the end of the day, your main keyword phrases must be chosen on the basis of relevance, and that is a function of judgment as much as data. You are the final arbiter as to whether a particular keyword phrase is pertinent to your book.

Stellar Tip:
If you're really stumped, use keyword phrases that use words like "Books" or "Guides."

Nonfiction example: "Infertility Guides"
Fiction example: "Vampire Books"

These types of keyword phrases are very popular on Amazon (they appear in almost every subject matter you can think of) but they have a big drawback: They're so general that they might not be of much help. In my example, "Flirting books" are way too broad for my book on flirt texting. Still, it's a starting point.

How To Squeeze Leading Indicators Out Of Amazon's Search Box.
Your job is to get Amazon's search box to cough up as many Leading Indicators as possible. I want to share a simple strategy that works quite well, though it requires epic patience: Use an A-Z approach to your keywords.

Let's take the example from my Flirty Tex Message Helper.

Step 1: Type in "how to text"
Step 2: Write down the relevant keyword phrases in the drop down menu. At the time of this writing they include...

How to text...
>   to speech
>   a girl
>   a guy
>   from your kindle
>   girls

Step 3: Now go through the alphabet. Type in "how to text a."

Step 4: Write down the relevant keyword phrases in the drop down menu. At the time of this writing they include...

How to text a...
>   Girl
>   Guy

Step 5: Continue with the alphabet. Type in "how to text b." Then, "how to text c," "how to text d," and so on. Keep repeating this until you get to the last letter in the alphabet (I believe it's "Z." Use your judgment).

Do this for every relevant keyword or keyword combination that makes sense for your book's topic. This is a time-consuming, patience-demanding process but in the end you will have a VERY good idea of how people are searching Amazon for books like yours.

Again, you have to bring your own personal judgment this process. Just because something shows up as a Leading Indicator doesn't mean you should use it. Make sure you type in different versions of your keywords, too. In my case, I typed in "flirt," "flirty," and "flirting." When I did that, Amazon's search box came up with a word I've never heard of: "Flirtexting." Magic!

Okay, so now you should have two lists:
1. The 20 or so keyword phrases you discovered on Google.
2. The Leading Indicator phrases you discovered on Amazon.

Now you need a third list: The 20 or so keyword phrases you discovered on Google that ALSO appear on Amazon's search box.

There's only one way to get that third list-- start typing the keyword phrases you discovered on Google into Amazon's search box. If they appear, you're golden. It means these are your main keyword phrases. If they don't, put them on your reserve list, as you still may be able to use them.

Google Keywords	Amazon Leading Indicators	Google Keywords Appearing on Amazon's Search Box
1.	1.	1.
2.	2.	2.
3.	3.	3.

Here's how I do it. I use an Excel spreadsheet (you can use any word processing document, really) and put the top 20 keyword phrases I find on Google on the left column, the Leading Indicators I find on Amazon in the middle and the keyword phrases that appear in both on the right.

Choose your top 12-15 keyword phrases from your three lists. You've got the data; now use your judgment. Remember the one question that should guide your decisions:

What keywords best describe the content of my book?

Spend some time on this. If you don't get this right it's hard to see how you're going to succeed. Remember, if Amazon's search spiders can't find you, neither will book buyers.

How To Get Your Book In Amazon's Top 10 Search Results.

You've just found out the keyword phrases readers use to find your type of book. Whenever a book buyer types these phrases into Amazon's search box, spiders go out and look for them in three different places: The title of your book, the description in your book page, and in the search profile Amazon asks you to fill out in the admin section.

Your objective is to now fill these three areas with the keyword phrases you just discovered. Again, they include:

1. The Title Of Your Book.

Never, EVER compromise the integrity of your book title to fit a keyword phrase into it. But if you can, you'll get a leg up on Amazon's search engine. This is quite difficult to do with fiction, but easily done in nonfiction. For tips on how to do it, turn to Chapter Three.

2. In The Search Profile Of Your Book's Account.

When you log into the admin section of your account, click the "Bookshelf" link and you'll see a section called, "Target Your Book To Customers." Amazon allows you to submit 7 keyword phrases that will help customers find you. These keywords will essentially be hotwired into the Amazon search engine, so choose carefully from your list of 12-15 and type them in. Write down the 7 keyword phrases and make sure you use them in your book description. You will rise much faster in the rankings if Amazon's search engine sees the same keyword phrases in different places.

3. The "Book Description" In Your Book's Landing Page.

Amazon gives you 4,000 characters (about 800 words) to describe your book. Inserting your keywords into this description is what's known as writing SEO copy (Search Engine Optimization). I show you how to do this in Chapter Eight. For now, just hold on to that all-important list of keyword phrases.

CHAPTER SIX

How To Pick The Right Categories For Your Book.

Amazon allows you to pick two "browse categories" for your book. Think of them as the section of the bookstore you'd like your book placed (literature, fiction, history, etc.). You can select up to two categories.

Categories are important because so many people use them to find the books they want. My goal is to get you into the Top 10 best sellers in a category. That may sound like a tall order but it's completely doable because Amazon has created bestseller lists for hundreds and hundreds of categories and sub-categories. While it may be next to impossible to break into the Top 10 of all books, it's entirely possible to break into the Top 10 for say, "Etiquette," as my book, Flirty Text Message Helper has done.

Once you get into the Top 10 of any category you're going to notice a self-perpetuating cycle of sales. There are two reasons for this:

1. Customers Browse The Categories Of Books They're Interested In.
Let's say you're looking for a book on texting. You found Michael Master's TextAppeal and read the book description. You're unsure about it but you notice in the "Product Details" section that it's in the following category:

Nonfiction > Reference > Etiquette

So you click on the "Etiquette" category link and it takes you to the top sellers in that category. Lo and behold, there's my book, The Flirty Text Message Helper at the #6 position. Your curiosity is up, you click on my cover and bam! The possibility of a sale.

2. Customers Purposefully Browse A Category They're Familiar With.
Some people know exactly what they want. If I've previously bought books in the etiquette category I may decide to check that category out to see what's new. I simply go here:

Kindle Home > Kindle ebooks > Nonfiction > Reference > Etiquette

Click on the Etiquette link and lo and behold, my book is there at rank #6. The cover and the title of my book intrigue you. You click on the cover and bam! Another possible sale.

If my book wasn't in the Top 10 you might not ever know about it (assuming you couldn't find it through keywords in the search box). Now, this isn't a zero sum game. It's not as if this self-perpetuating sales dynamic doesn't occur if you're ranked #19 instead of #1. It's just that the association between number of sales and category ranking gets stronger and stronger as you get to the top.

Of course, there's the chicken and the egg question: Are your sales improving because you made the Top 10 in a category or did you make the Top 10 because your sales improved?

The answer is both. Obviously, you can only get into a Top 10 if your sales improve, but once you're on that list it tends to perpetuate your sales.

As you can see, getting into a Top 10 in a category is a powerful way of selling books. So the question is, which category should you be in? The truth is that over time, Amazon will put you into the category it sees fit (their algorithm slots you into a category by looking at how buyers tend to find you. Sometimes these categories are ridiculous but once Amazon decides you don't have a choice). However, you do have a choice to decide which categories you want to be in for the first few months. And if you make it to the Top 10 in those categories Amazon will leave you alone.

How To Decide Which Categories Your Book Should Be In.

First, familiarize yourself with Amazon's categories by going into your admin section. You'll notice a dizzying array of categories and subcategories. In fact, there are so many they'll make you reach for the aspirin. Obviously, I can't tell you which subcategory you should try because I don't know the nature of your book, but I've got a few guidelines you should follow:

Find out which categories your competition is in.
Pick out the books you feel are most like yours. Make a list of the different subcategories they're listed under. Click on them to see who is in the Top 10 or Top 20. Familiarize yourself with the categories so you can make an informed decision.

Determine the number of book sales in the category you're considering.
There's no point in putting your book in a category where the #1 book sells a unit every other day. You want to be a big fish in a small pond, not a puddle. By the same token, you don't want to be in a category dominated by the super

sellers (you'll never crack it). So how do you decide on a subcategory that's profitable enough to be in, but not so big you can't crack it? Let's use my Flirty Text Message Helper as an example.

I didn't want to be in the broad dating category because there were too many blockbusters in there. I have no illusions about my book—it's no best seller, but I also know that it's a useful book for a lot of people. So, I wanted a category that no blockbuster would ever dwell in. I noticed that one of my competitors was in the "Etiquette" section. That struck me odd, but hey, I say follow the market because the market won't follow you.

I then created a chart of the top ten sellers in the Etiquette category, and using the sales rank-to-units-sold ratios you'll see in Chapter 14, I got a real good sense of the subcategory's viability. At the time of this writing, the Top 10 books in the "Etiquette" subcategory had the following sales rank/units sold:

Book Rank	Overall Sales Rank	Category Rank	Est # of Daily Books Sold
Better Than Beauty	5,669	1	21
Art Of Manliness	6,935	2	18
How To Get The Girl	7,151	3	15
The Art of Manliness II	8,150	4	12
The Bro Code	11,383	5	9
TextAppeal	18,086	6	7
The Texting Bible	19,137	7	5
How To Be Hepburn	24,586	8	5
1001 Conversation Starters	26,260	9	5
Emily Post's Etiquette	27,559	10	3

As you can see, this is the perfect category for a small book like Flirty Text Message Helper: No blockbusters but enough revenue to make it worthwhile. I entered the subcategory and using the principles you're reading in this book hit the Top 10 in the Etiquette category in a matter of about a month (as of this writing I'm hovering around #6 in the Top 10). That's about seven books a day (49 a week, 210 a month). Not bad, for a simple, 30-page listing of funny texts, no?

Remember, Amazon allows you to choose two categories, so get cracking. Prepare yourself for a little confusion, Amazon-style. You're going to see some of your competitors in a few screwy categorizations. For example, the best seller, Why Men Love Bitches. It's in the dating subcategory, but look at its parent category:

Books > Health, Fitness & Dieting > Relationships > Dating

Why Amazon would categorize a best selling dating book under Health, Fitness & Dieting is beyond the purview of mere mortals like myself. How do I know the publisher didn't intentionally put it there? Because if you go into your admin section and click on Health, Fitness & Dieting, there's no "Relationships" or "Dating" category!

I'll be honest. Amazon's categories are a hot mess. The best you can do is choose the category in the admin section that best matches the category in the "storefront" that consumers see. Again, the categories in the admin section DO NOT necessarily match the categories that consumers ultimately see. Choose the best fitting categories, keep watching your book and its competitors and see if maybe there's a better category for you to be in (it's not unusual for Amazon to add or subtract categories since you were last in the admin section!).

For a fuller explanation of Amazon's categories I turned to Aaron Shepard, Amazon wunderkind, developer of the gee-whiz Sales Ranking Express (helps track your sales ranking across all of Amazon's domestic and international sites) and author of Aiming At Amazon (I highly recommend it for peeps interested in Publishing On Demand). Here's what he told me:

> "The reason the categories on the KDP form don't match the Amazon categories [what consumers see] is because KDP is using industry-standard BISAC categories. And the reason they change is that the BISAC categories are revised yearly. You can find them here:
>
> http://www.bisg.org/what-we-do-cat-20-classification-schemes.php
>
> So, you're classifying your book in BISAC, then Amazon maps those categories to its own. This method makes sense, because it relieves Amazon of having to provide a relatively stable scheme for the submissions of KDP publishers. Meanwhile, both the Amazon categories and the mapping can change at any time, and as you point out, sometimes the results are weird. Still, you can map the conversions yourself by experimenting with what shows up when you choose specific BISAC categories."

Increasing Sales Through "Category Leapfrogging."
You can dramatically increase your sales by getting into the top 10 of a small category and then leaping over to a bigger category. For example, I had a dating book that hit the top 10 under a "Relationships" subcategory. When I switched it to the "Sex" category, sales increased by 30%! Same book, different category, stunning results. The trick here, as stated before, is to navigate the confusing structure of Amazon's categories.

You don't have to reach a top 10 list before you switch categories, by the way. If your book isn't doing well, it might behoove you to switch categories early on. Take this book, for example. I initially placed it in two categories—Home-Based Businesses and Entrepreneurial. It did decently enough. My average sales ranking hovered around the 15,000 – 20,000 range. One day I noticed an indirect competitor on my "Customers Who Bought This..." section that was doing quite well. He was in a category I had initially rejected—Writing Skills. It didn't make sense for me to be in there because my book isn't about how to write but how to sell what you write. Still, I began to think things through. No, my book isn't about writing but the only people who look in the Writing Skills are writers—people who have books or are in the process of writing them. In other words, MY TARGET AUDIENCE. So I switched categories. Within about a week my sales ranking shot up to as high as 1,500. At the time of this writing (three months later) it hovers in the 2,500 range.

Changing categories took my book from OK to OMG. I don't want to make switching categories sound like a miracle because I've done it for my other books and didn't always see such stunning results. Still, it's important that you constantly question the categories you chose and be on the lookout for other opportunities.

Important Tip: Do not change categories (or any aspect of your marketing) until you appear on page 1 or 2 of Amazon's search engine for your keyword phrases. Otherwise, you may be trying to solve the wrong problem. If people can't find you on Amazon's search engine, it's highly doubtful they're going to find you because you changed categories. If you do your SEO right, it should take you about four weeks to start appearing on page 1 or 2.

Notes

_____

_____

_____

_____

_____

_____

_____

_____

_____

_____

_____

_____

_____

_____

_____

_____

_____

_____

_____

_____

_____

_____

_____

_____

_____

_____

_____

_____

CHAPTER SEVEN

How To Put A Billboard For Your Book On Your Competitors' Pages.

A friend once called me a liar. Another friend rose to my defense and said I was not a liar, but I got more mileage out of the truth than anyone he'd ever met. So when I say there are ethical ways of using your competitors to catapult you into a Top 10 category, I'm not lying. I'm saying I get 100 MPG.

Let me tell you a story. For three months, my ebook, The Flirty Text Message Helper, languished on Kindle. Wracking my brains, I looked at competitive books that were doing well in its category. Specifically, Michael Master's *TextAppeal*, Vanessa Taylor's *Text, Love, Power* and the biggest dating blockbuster of the last five years, Sherry Argov's *Why Men Love Bitches*.

I looked at their "Customers Who Bought This Item Also Bought..." section and was overcome by Association Envy. If I could get the buyers of these books to buy mine, then Amazon would put it in their "Customers Who Bought" section. And then, my book would really take off.

But how could I do that? I tried to do it artificially by buying their books and then buying mine. It didn't work. You have to buy an enormous number of books to get an association with a category bestseller.

As I scoured my competitor's pages I noticed the Reviews section. The left side is dominated by three or four "big" reviews—the ones designated as "Most Helpful" by other browsers. They are printed in their entirety. But look to your right. You'll see ten truncated reviews in the "Most Recent Customer Reviews." Each review has four lines before it ends with a "Read More" link.

Now, what would happen if I could get a friend to write a useful review of my competitor's book with a clickable link to my own? And made sure that the link was visible before the review got cut off by "Read More"? It would look something like this...

Most Recent Customer Reviews

★★★★★ Great guide for people like me who freeze when they get a flirty text

After getting some great texting ideas from The Flirty Text Message Helper: Witty Texts For Clever People (great book, I highly recommend it)I realized I had a bigger problem than...

Read more

Published 4 minutes ago by Carol Fulwiler Jones, MA

When you click on "Read More" the review expands to this:

★★★★★ **Great guide for people like me who freeze when they get a flirty text**, July 26, 2012

By **Carol Fulwiler Jones, MA** - See all my reviews

(Edit review) (Delete review)

This review is from: **TextAppeal - For Girls! - The Ultimate Texting Guide (Kindle Edition)**

After getting some great texting ideas from The Flirty Text Message Helper: Witty Texts For Clever People (great book, I highly recommend it)I realized I had a bigger problem than what to write. It was how to get and keep a guy's attention (sadly, not every guy that texts me is as interested as I am in them).

So here's what the author does best: He shows you how to build attraction through the use of anticipation and suspense. That is an art form in itself, but especially in a relatively new medium like texting. Texting is more like tweeting than emailing. You must think in sound bites and approach every interaction as if it were a mini-episode in a TV series. Meaning, create "cliff hangers" so the audience wants to tune in to the next episode. This book will show you how to do it.

Tension is oxygen to attraction. The author's genius is in helping you create it and build it so that the guys you're interested in will a) ask you out b) fall in love.

Here's what happened. Two weeks after that review appeared in the right hand corner of my competitor's book, TextAppeal, my book showed up in its "Customers Who Bought This Item Also Bought..." section. Sales skyrocketed.

Why did it work? As the "newest" review, my friend's review rose to the very top of TextAppeal's "Most Recent Customer Reviews" and stayed in the section until it got pushed off the page with newer reviews. I literally put a billboard of my book in my competitors' book pages!

And because I chose a long-established best seller that wasn't getting many new reviews, it took about four weeks before I got pushed off the page. Plenty of time to get my foot in the door and let my competitor do the selling for me.

I tell you this story so that you can learn...

How To Get Into Your Competitor's "Customers Who Bought This Item Also Bought..." Section

Step 1: Pick three complementary books whose association will do you the most good. You're looking for best sellers that complement the content of your book. In my example, I chose to review TextAppeal, a guide to texting. We're not really competitors since his book is a guide and mine is a collection of texts. Anybody who buys a texting guide like TextAppeal is going to be interested in funny, flirty texts they can call their own. I also picked two dating books that sold very well, but were at least six months old: *Text. Love. Power* and *Why Men Love Bitches.*

Unignorable Tip: Choose books that complement yours AND have scale. There's no point in getting associated with a book that doesn't sell well.

Step 2: Get a friend to write the review. Do NOT do it yourself.
Posting a link to your book in a review of a competitive book is against Amazon's Terms Of Service. They will eventually get wise to you and remove the review under cover of darkness. They'll match the ASIN number of the book link to the account posting the review and take it down. One morning you will wake up and poof! Your review will be gone. You'll also get a gentle reminder to refrain from doing it again. Why doesn't Amazon allow it? Because they know links result in sales! And if they allow competitors to post links on each other's reviews their site would like spam-bots colonized it.

Still, Amazon wants people to post links in their reviews and encourages them to do it with easy-to-follow directions. Why? *Because they know links result in sales!* They just don't want authors linking to their own books. Your job is to recruit friends to do the linking for you. The instructions to follow are directed at your friend...

Step 3: Write a positive review for the selected books.
Don't trash competitors (especially when you're using them as a sales trampoline). If the book sucks, then just focus on the good parts. The review doesn't have to be very long—less than 200 words. Here is my friend's review of TextAppeal:

> After getting some great texting ideas from The Flirty Text Message Helper: Witty Texts For Clever People (great book, I highly recommend it) I realized I had a bigger problem than what to write. It was how to get and keep a guy's attention (sadly, not every guy that texts me is as interested as I am in them).
>
> So here's what the author does best: He shows you how to build attraction through the use of anticipation and suspense. That is an art form in itself, but especially in a relatively new medium like texting. Texting is more like tweeting than emailing. You must think in sound bites and approach every interaction as if it were a mini-episode in a TV series. Meaning, create "cliff hangers" so the audience wants to tune in to the next episode. This book will show you how to do it.
>
> Tension is oxygen to attraction. The author's genius is in helping you create it and build it so that the guys you're interested in will a) ask you out b) fall in love.

A couple of points about the reviews:

- Make sure you have a grabby headline.
- Make it helpful, useful, and insightful. You don't want to stain your friend's book or their reputation with a badly written review.
- Do NOT sell your friend's book. Mention it once and only once, and not in a sell context.

Step 4: Mention the title of the book in the first sentence.
Amazon allows about 30 words or 176 characters (with spaces) before they cut off the review with a "Read More" link. The whole point of this exercise is for browsers who are scanning these reviews to notice YOUR book. Few will click the "Read More" link, so you've got to put the title of your book in the first sentence or two. It's going to stand out in bold blue because you will...

Step 5: Put a clickable link to your book.
This will take the browser directly to your book page. Pretty swell, huh? Here are the steps to inserting a hyperlink to your book:

- Click the "Create Your Own Review" button on your competitor's page. You'll be taken to a text box where you can enter the review.

- Write your review.
  Remember, be nice! And write it well.

- Position the cursor where you want the link to your book.
  You don't actually write out the name of your book. Amazon will do that for you. Just position the insertion point in the right location for now. It should be right after a phrase like, "As the author of."

- Click the "Insert Product Link Here" button.
  It will open to a "Select A Product" Search box. Toggle to "Kindle Store." Type in the name of your book. Click on the cover of your book.

You're done. And done.

One Click Only.
Amazon allows you up to ten links in a review but it would be foolish for you to put in more than one. Remember, you're not "selling" your book here; you're inviting people to click over. And speaking of clicking over, the "billboarding" technique I've just described is yet another reason to come up with an irresistible title for your book. My book title isn't irresistible, but what it lacks in engagement it makes up in specificity. If you're into flirt texting, it's hard not to click on it.

Notes

ENGAGE: HOW TO GENERATE SERIOUS INTEREST IN YOUR BOOK.

CHAPTER EIGHT

How To Write Oceanfront Book Descriptions.

In real estate terms, your "Book Description" should read like an oceanfront home. Yet, most read like a trailer on cinder blocks. They're either filled with a few paragraphs of half-hearted pablum, overloaded with the hyperbole of an infomercial or misted with vague, unsatisfying copy that fails to convert. Which is strange, because...

Packaging Is Everything.
Nobody actually reads much of a book before buying it. Sales reps convince store buyers with covers and a few paragraphs of catalog copy. Same with wholesalers and distributors. Consumers don't read much of the books they buy, either. They base most of their decision on cover, title, subject matter, author, jacket copy and a few glances at the actual content. Almost all buying decisions, up and down the line, are made on the title, cover design and the accompanying sales copy.

If You Don't Give Good Copy You Won't Get Good Sales.
Think about your own browsing on Amazon. A cover caught your eye. The title seems intriguing. You've never heard of the author and there are no credible book reviews. You only have two ways of judging it: Read the book description or click the "Look Inside" Button. Which will you do first? Read the description, of course. What if you don't like it? You won't "Look Inside" and you certainly won't click the buy button. You just lost the sale.

Let's open up the skull of a potential buyer and see what kind of doubts and objections he or she has when they land on a poorly written book description:

- I'm not sure what this book is about.
- This book does not solve my problem (nonfiction).
- I don't get a complete sense of the characters or the story lines (fiction).
- It doesn't seem to deliver what's promised in the cover or title.
- If the level of writing in the description reflects the level of writing in the book, I'll take a pass.
- I'm not sure what I'll get out of this book.
- The book description leaves me flat.
- There's not enough information for me to make a decision.
- I don't like the way this book is described.

If you can answer these objections you've probably got the sale. Now, I'm not going to lie, writing copy to sell your book may be the most difficult thing a writer can do. Most of us are too emotionally involved with our work to be able to see it with fresh eyes. For that reason, hiring a copywriter may be a clear-eyed option for you. If it costs too much (I don't know many writers who can afford it, truthfully) then listen closely. You're about to find out how to create some emotional distance from your work and write a description that overcomes sales-killing obstacles.

First, let's handle the thought that stops you from writing sales copy:

> *"I shouldn't have to sell the book; it should sell itself."*

No book sells itself. Yours included. Yours especially. As an unknown author, good sales copy is your only way out of oblivion. The best way to get over your hesitation is to make sure you've got the right hat on when you begin. See, you shouldn't be writing the book description as the author. You should be writing it as the publisher. An author writes on his own terms. The publisher writes to the customers' desires. The author is content-motivated; the publisher is marketing-driven. Once I'm done writing my books I take off my author hat and put on my publisher's sombrero. Here's the process I use to get that "oceanfront view":

Part 1: Research.
Read the book descriptions of your closest competitors. Which ones make you want to buy them? Why? Take notes. Don't be afraid of using their techniques. Remember, originality is the art of concealing your sources.

Part 2: Answer These Questions.
Fiction:
- What is the Big Problem or central conflict?
- Who are the main characters?
- What are their goals, their mission?
- What are they trying to accomplish?
- What is the catalyst/presenting problem?
- Who or what are the biggest obstacles the main character has to face?
- What is at stake?
- What is the heart of the story?
- What's the hook?
- What's the setting?
- What is the primary action that drives the story?
- What is the emotional core?
- What are the external conflicts (the world is coming to an end!)

- What are the internal conflicts (torn between two lovers)
- What is the driving emotional force? (revenge, love)
- Will they succeed? (introduce doubt)

Nonfiction How-To:

- What problem do you solve?
- How will you solve it?
- What are the underlying issues?
- What's at stake if the reader doesn't solve his or her problem?
- What's the benefit of buying the book?
- What will readers learn that they don't know already?
- What's the implicit/explicit promise?
- Why are you qualified to write about this?
- Have you demonstrated empathy for the reader and their problem?
- Have you clearly identified all aspects of the problem you're trying to solve?
- Have you identified the obstacles that stop people from realizing their goals?
- What are your readers currently doing wrong that buying the book would correct?
- Have you given examples?

Part 3: Write The First Draft.

Amazon gives you 4,000 characters (about 800 words). Be specific. Use strong nouns. Punchy verbs. No adjectives. Don't sell. Tease. Entice. Excite. Don't start off by saying something like, "This is a coming-of-age story that..." It's the equivalent of starting a book with, "It was a dark and stormy night." Don't tell us about the story. Tell us the story itself.

There are two ways to describe a married couple's fight. You can stand outside their house and tell me what's going or you can throw open the curtains and let me watch. Satisfy the voyeur in your potential customers. Here are some tips that'll keep you on the right track:

• Write the book description in third person and present tense. As if you're sitting face-to-face with a browser who just asked you what the book is about.

• Try not to mention more than three or four characters unless they're vital to the story. If you can't hook them with four characters you won't be able to do it with five or six.

• Don't include subplots. Stick to the main plot or main theme.

• Use power words to evoke emotions. Words like tormented, charismatic, or ruthless have the power to catapult readers into a different state of mind. Use them. Search "Power words" on Google and you'll find plenty of them. Or buy Richard Bayan's classic, Words That Sell.

• Mirror the pace and tone of the book. A thriller, for example, should have pulse-quickening language.

• Command the reader's attention from the very first line. Remember, the job of the first line in your book description is to get the second line read. The job of the second line is to get the third line read (and so on).

• Use words associated with your genre. If your book's a mystery, use words such as "suspicious" and "investigation." If there are paranormal elements use words like "demon" or "worlds colliding." If it's a nonfiction business book, use buzzwords.

• Come up with a memorable tagline. Often called slogans, taglines are catchy, enticing short phrases that sum up the plot, tone or themes of a book. You see it in movies all the time. Take Alien, for example: "In Space, No One Can Hear You Scream." Here's one I love for fiction—it's for Family Pack, a novel about werewolves: "Some Family Curses Are Worth Passing On."

Part 4: Delete All Adjectives And Adverbs.
Adjectives and adverbs are hyperbole's henchmen. Delete, delete, delete. Readers are more sophisticated than the average person. They know when they're being manipulated. Remember, throw open the curtains and let me see in. I don't need your adjectives—I've got eyes of my own.

Part 5: Insert Reviews And Blurbs From Credible Sources.
If a well-known blog, website or magazine has reviewed your book, stick it in there. If somebody famous or semi-famous said something nice about it, stick it in there, too. They'll go a long way to establishing credibility and offering "buyer's insurance" that your book just may well be worth the money. Just use them sparingly. Remember, Amazon limits you to about 650 words. Every word you use in a review is a word you have to take out of describing the book.

Part 6: Add A "Personal Note From The Author" If Appropriate.
This can be an effective tool if you have a compelling personal connection to the book. For example, the author of Managing The Stress Of Infertility has a "Personal Note" section because she too went through the trials and tribulations of infertility treatments. In the end, customers are taking a chance on you. Give them a personal reason to buy your book if you have an appropriate one.

Part 7: Optimize The Book Description For Amazon's Search Engine By Integrating Your Most Important Keyword Phrases.
You are writing the description of your book for two audiences: Humans and Amazon's search engine. Humans need captivating language; searchbots feed on keywords. Tilt it completely to the human side and Amazon's engine might never find you. Tilt it to the search engine and customers won't buy you (stilted language is sales kryptonite). SEO copy is the art of blending in keyword phrases so they attract search engines without turning off customers.

Let's take stock of where we are. By now, you should have written an oceanfront view description. Now it's time to blend in the keyword phrases. Resist the urge to stuff. Most beginners think they can game the system by bloating their book description with keyword after keyword. Don't do it. It's unclear if Amazon follows the policies of other search engines like Google and Yahoo, but I'd bet an unsolicited shoulder rub that they too penalize any landing page that looks like a keyword stuffed abomination.

The penalty isn't just that Amazon's search engine will drop you to the bottom of its results pages; it's that even if customers find you, they won't buy you. Not if you sound like an endlessly repeating infomercial.

So how do you write great SEO copy? How do you finesse your keywords in so that customers don't notice them but Amazon does? Here are the steps:

1. Identify your top 12-15 keyword phrases.
Use the list that you developed in Chapter Five.

2. Look for generic words that can be replaced with a keyword phrase.
For example, in Managing The Stress Of Infertility we switched a single generic word—"book"—into a keyword phrase ("infertility guide"). We started out with this...

Pregnancy Issues Addressed In This Book:
And ended up with this...
Pregnancy Issues Addressed In This Infertility Guide:

3. Create opportunities to use keywords naturally.
We knew that "infertility treatment" was a massive keyword for us, so we invented ways of using it that felt natural. For instance, we came up with a simple question: *Are You In Treatment for Infertility?*

As a postscript, you should know that search engines give points to keywords within the same sentence, even if they don't follow each other sequentially. In other words, "infertility treatment" is just as valuable as "treatment for infertility." This gives you a lot more maneuvering room in the way you use keywords.

4. Insert punctuation or line breaks between the words in any given phrase. Search engines ignore basic punctuation and line breaks, so they see the keyword phrase as if it were intact. For example, Amazon will recognize our keyword phrase "infertility treatment" even when we separate the words with punctuation:

"Many women struggle with **infertility. Treatment** is the last thing they want."

5. Use subheads.
Sometimes it is hard to slot a keyword phrase in naturally. That's where subtitles come in. They're a great way to add a phrase without calling attention to it. We knew "infertility cure" was a strong keyword phrase but there was no credible way to put it in the copy, so we put it in a subtitle. Example:

> **Special Section For Women Seeking An <u>Infertility Cure</u>.**
> Learn how to turn 'required sex' into passionate loving by igniting desire, dealing with mismatched libidos, and learning sexual positions and techniques that won't hurt your ovaries when they're enlarged and painful.

6. Don't use the same keyword phrase more than three times.
It's better to go wide than deep. You'll be more effective using 15 different keywords once than five keywords three times over. This is because search engines value different phrasings of the same keywords over pure repetition.

7. Aim for a 3-5% keyword density. In other words, out of 650 words, approximately 19-30 should be words that are part of a keyword phrase. Assuming the average keyword phrase is 2.5 words long, that means you should use between 7 to 12 keyword phrases on your page.

Here is the complete description for my client's book, *Managing The Stress Of Infertility*. It's filled with keyword phrases (underlined) without sounding like they were handed out like flyers at a rally:

> **Are You In Treatment For Infertility?**
>
> Do you get upset when you attend baby showers or go to malls full of baby strollers and pregnant women?
>
> Do you feel like crying when friends or family ask a question like, "Are you still <u>trying to get pregnant</u>?"
>
> Do you wish your husband would be more supportive and take a more active role in your fertility and conception treatments?

Are you spending too much time worrying about becoming pregnant?

Do you feel like your body has betrayed you every time you start your period?

Do you feel helpless, powerless, and out of control?

This Infertility Book Will Help You:
- Manage Your Emotions
- Get Your Husband To Be More Supportive And Involved
- Deal With Painful Social Situations
- Ease Your Frustrations
- Regain A Sense Of Control.

Issues About Fertility And Pregnancy Addressed In My Managing The Stress Of Infertility Guide:
- Handling The Disappointment Of Getting Your Period
- How To Stop Feeling You Have No Control Over Your Body (Especially With Infertility PCOS)
- How To Deal With Insensitive Comments, Unwanted Advice, And Unwelcome Questions
- How To Deal With Painful Questions Like, "How Many Children Do You Have?" Or "Are You Trying To Get Pregnant?"
- How To Decide Whether You Should Tell Friends And Family That You're Seeking Fertility Treatment. (And What To Say)

My Anti-Stress Fertility Guide Also Shows You How To Deal With Difficult Situations Like...
- A Girlfriend Calling To Say She's Pregnant
- Whether You Should Attend Baby Showers
- Getting Your Husband To Be More Understanding & Supportive
- Keeping Yourself Emotionally Safe During Holidays

Special Section For Women Seeking An Infertility Cure:
How To Turn "Required" Sex Into Passionate Loving
Increase your interest in sex, deal with mismatched libidos, and learn sexual positions and techniques that won't hurt your ovaries when they're enlarged and painful.

Special Section For Women Seeking Infertility Meditations:
Breathing Practices To Decrease Your Stress, Shift Your Energy, And Manage The Physical Demands Of Trying To Get Pregnant.

A step-by-step program for five kinds of conscious breathing practices.

What The Experts Say About Managing The Stress Of Infertility:

"While Carol Jones' own journey with infertility is the heart and soul that nurtured this book, it is her professional expertise and long experience counseling couples facing the challenges of infertility that make it such a valuable resource for others."
—*Carrell Dammann, PhD, Family Psychologist, Open House, Inc., Atlanta, GA*

"A concise and practical book that helps couples lighten the emotional burden that accompanies infertility."
—*Linda Applegarth, EdD, Director of Psychological Services, Perelman/Cohen Center for Reproductive Medicine, Weill-Cornell University Medical College, New York, NY*
"Carol Jones has written an insightful and helpful roadmap to managing emotions and relationships through a fertility journey. She blends her personal experience and professional expertise in a way that is easy to grasp and emulate."
—*Dan Shapiro, MD, Director of Egg Donation Services, Reproductive Biology Associates, Atlanta, GA*

A Personal Note From The Author:
This book blends 20 years of my experience as a psychotherapist counseling hundreds of women <u>trying to get pregnant</u>, with my own personal experiences as a woman who sought <u>infertility treatments</u>.

I know the emotions around trying to conceive are sometimes more challenging than the <u>infertility treatments</u> themselves. I used to torture myself with questions like, "What have I done to cause my infertility?" I felt like crying when I saw pregnant women and baby strollers.

That's why I've put together this step-by-step <u>infertility guide</u>. It will heal the pain, ease the frustration, and help you regain a sense of control. It is my intention to keep you emotionally safe until you become pregnant.

Part 8: Use HTML Coding In Chapter Eight To Make The Page Look Vibrant.
Now that you've provided an oceanfront view to your book, don't you think it could use a little landscaping? Using formatting (headlines, color, pictures, and bold, italicized or underlined words) is the equivalent of turning a dirt yard into a blooming garden. With HTML, the page comes

alive, looks professional and guides the consumer's eyes to the most salient aspects of the book. Learn how to do it in Chapter Eight.

Use All Of Amazon's Word Count.

Somebody once asked me to identify the most common mistake people make on their book description page. Writing short copy is right up there with the worst offenses. I am always amazed at how many writers think they can sell their book with just a few paragraphs. Amazon allows you 4,000 characters (about 800 words), yet time and again I see book descriptions with just a fraction of the allowable number.

Short book descriptions sharply decrease the chances of a sale or even a click on the Look Inside feature because they don't give enough information to motivate next-step actions. I don't know how many times I've seen a short book description and thought, "I don't know what this book is about and I'll be damned if I'm going to click on the Look Inside feature to find out." Talk about a lost sale!

Don't make the mistake of thinking that you can convey the features and benefits of your book in a hundred and fifty words, the way print books do on their jacket covers. Stephen King can get away with it; you and I can't. Use all 4,000 characters Amazon provides. You'll know if you've done a good job if you end up cursing Amazon for being so chintzy with their character count.

Remind People To Use The Look Inside Feature.

Years of selling PDF downloads taught me never to assume that what's obvious to me is obvious to my customers. For example, it may be obvious (to me) that customers should click on the Look Inside button after reading an engaging book description, but it may not be obvious to them. That's why I ask them to do it in my sales copy. You'd think you wouldn't have to say something so obvious but you do. Here's a great example of why it pays to be prescriptive: Once, before I knew better than to market outside Kindle's ecosystem, I tried to advertise my books on a dating website. They rejected the banner ads for my books because they didn't say, "Click Here." I objected, telling the ad manager I didn't want to junk up the ad with an appallingly obvious instruction. "Everybody knows to click on an ad banner if they're interested," I said. Unmoved, the manager replied, "We've done the research--ads that say 'Click Here' get twice the response rate." I believed him because I knew his organization doesn't make a policy move that isn't backed up by yards and yards of research data.

It seems counter-intuitive, but if you don't remind people to do the painfully obvious they often won't do it. It isn't always possible to invite people to "scroll up and click the Look Inside feature on the top left hand side of the page" but you should seriously consider it. Don't assume anything. Some people aren't aware the Look Inside feature exists, some people forget to use it, and some are too distracted to think about it. A gentle reminder can be the difference between silence and the ring of a cash register.

Should You Write Your Book Description On Author Central Or The General Admin Page?

There are two ways you can enter your book description copy: Through Author Central or the general admin page, officially called the KDP or Kindle Direct Publishing (https://kdp.amazon.com). It is a lot easier to do it through Author Central but I think it's a very bad idea. Let me explain why:

1. *Author Central dramatically reduces the book description's allowable word count by 40%.*

If you go through KDP you get 4,000 characters or 800 words in your book description. If you go through Author Central you get 2,400 characters or 480 words. Holy flying feces, Batman! That's a huge decrease. A word count reduction of 40% is completely unacceptable. The book description is too critical to take a hit like that. Not only do you weaken your ability to communicate the book's worth, you'll do severe damage to your SEO. You'd literally have to cut your keyword phrases by 40%! You may as well stick your butt in the basement and kiss it goodbye with a premium hand rolled cigar.

2. *Once you change your book's description via Author Central you can't change it via KDP.*

That means you'll be forever stuck with 480 words in your description with no hope of ever changing it back to 800 without completely starting from scratch. Nobody knows why Amazon provides such a wildly different word count between the two access points but I suspect it's an infrastructure issue.

3. *Author Central won't let you use pictures in the book description.*

The HTML code for loading pictures (Chapter Nine) will work if you go through KDP but not through Author Central. Pictures are a great way of dressing your book page. Why rob yourself of this competitive advantage?

Bottom line: Place your book description through KDP rather than Author Central. There is just no advantage other than convenience to do otherwise.

Placing Other Copy Through Author Central.
Author Central allows you to write a ton of copy in sections that appear below the "Customers Who Bought..." section. Take a look:

Section	Character Count	Word Count
Editorial Reviews	1,750 characters	(350 words)
Product Description	2,400 characters	(480 words)
From The Author	8,000 characters	(1,600 words)
From The Inside Flap	8,000 characters	(1,600 words)
From The Back Cover	8,000 characters	(1,600 words)
About The Author	2,000 characters	(400 words)

That's a lot of copy. It adds up to 6,030 words above and beyond the 800 you've (hopefully) put into your book description. This is a terrible idea! You can't use that much copy without making your book page look like a rock concert just let out.

It isn't just the length of the copy that bothers me as much as where that copy is placed—below the section called "Customers Who Bought This Item Also Bought..." You have to understand something about this section: It's a competitive threat. It is quite literally an ad campaign to get people to buy your competitor's books. If you haven't sold me by the time Amazon advertises your competitor's books, there's very little likelihood that copy underneath the advertising is going to help.

Think about how you came to buy this book. Many of you originally saw it in a competitor's "Customers Who Bought This..." section. Why did you click on my book instead of buying the one you just read about? Because the book description you were reading wasn't good enough and when Amazon presented you with other options, you took it.

You must get prospects to buy or click on your Look Inside feature BEFORE Amazon tempts them with your competitors or your sales are going to be locked in the basement so long they're going to put your book cover on a milk carton.

The "Customers Who Bought" section is a threshold analogous to the crease that runs across the middle of newspapers when they're folded up. Editors know that stories "above the fold" are far more likely to get read than stories "below the fold." Only it's worse on Amazon because it's not about reading; it's about buying. If you can't persuade book buyers with copy "above the fold" you are inviting them to click on your competitors. It is highly doubtful that copy "below the fold" is going to change their minds.

The Exceptions To The Rule.

You might want to consider using some of the additional copy sections available in Author Central if:

a)   You have third-party reviews you'd like to showcase (newspapers, magazines, blogs, etc). Put them in the section called Editorial Reviews.

b)   You have an engaging Q&A that can shed light on you, your characters or the book as a whole. Tread carefully. Most Q&A's I've seen look like the hack P.R. stunts that they are. But I've seen many that got me closer to a buy click. I think they work particularly well if your book is part of a series. Put them in the From The Author or Product Description section.

Examples Of Great Book Descriptions—Fiction.

You've seen how to execute a solid book description page for a nonfiction book. What about fiction? Below you'll see some examples. They are too short in my opinion, but they illustrate how well you can describe your book:

From Living Dead In Dallas, by Charlaine Harris:
"Cocktail waitress Sookie Stackhouse is on a streak of bad luck. First, her coworker is murdered and no one seems to care. Then she's face-to-face with a beastly creature that gives her a painful and poisonous lashing. Enter the vampires, who graciously suck the poison from her veins (like they didn't enjoy it). Point is, they saved her life. So when one of the blood-suckers asks for a favor, she complies. And soon, Sookie's in Dallas using her telepathic skills to search for a missing vampire. She's supposed to interview certain humans involved. There's just one condition: The vampires must promise to behave–and let the humans go unharmed. Easier said than done. All it takes is one delicious blonde and one small mistake for things to turn deadly..."

From The Phoenix Apostles, by Lynn Sholes and Joe Moore:
"Magazine journalist Seneca Hunt is reporting on the opening of Montezuma's tomb in Mexico City when the dig team, led by her fiancé Daniel Bernal, learns that the remains of the Aztec emperor are missing. Within moments of the discovery, an apparent terrorist attack kills everyone at the site—including Daniel. Seneca barely escapes the carnage.

Determined to get answers, Seneca starts investigating. She finds out that someone is stealing the remains of the most infamous mass murderers in history—and plotting to slaughter millions in the name of an ancient cult. Teaming up with bestselling novelist Matt Everhart, Seneca tries to stay one step ahead of those who want her dead as she and Matt follow a deadly 2000-year-old trail that leads back to the death of Jesus Christ."

From The Outlander by Gil Adamson:
In 1903 Mary Boulton flees alone across the West, one heart-pounding step ahead of the law. At nineteen, she has just become a widow-and her husband's killer. As bloodhounds track her frantic race toward the mountains, she is tormented by mad visions and by the knowledge that her two ruthless brothers-in-law are in pursuit, determined to avenge their younger brother's death. Responding to little more than the primitive instinct for survival at any cost, she retreats ever deeper into the wilderness-and into the wilds of her own mind.

The Detachment, by Barry Eisler:
When legendary black ops veteran Colonel Scott "Hort" Horton tracks Rain down in Tokyo, Rain can't resist the offer: a multi-million dollar payday for the "natural causes" demise of three ultra-high-profile targets who are dangerously close to launching a coup in America.

But the opposition on this job is going to be too much for even Rain to pull it off alone. He'll need a detachment of other deniable irregulars: his partner, the former Marine sniper, Dox. Ben Treven, a covert operator with ambivalent motives and conflicted loyalties. And Larison, a man with a hair trigger and a secret he'll kill to protect.

From the shadowy backstreets of Tokyo and Vienna, to the deceptive glitz and glamour of Los Angeles and Las Vegas, and finally to a Washington, D.C. in a permanent state of war, these four lone wolf killers will have to survive presidential hit teams, secret CIA prisons, and a national security state as obsessed with guarding its own secrets as it is with invading the privacy of the populace. But first, they'll have to survive each other.

Notes

CHAPTER NINE

Formatting Your Book Description To Look Like A Million Bucks.

Revealed! The HTML coding secrets that Amazon doesn't want you to know.

Ask Apple Computers if design sells. Then ask yourself if a well-designed book page wouldn't do the same.

I can tell you for a fact it does. When I introduced color, headlines, and font styles like bold, italics, underline and strikethroughs to my book pages, my sales popped by 20-30% in just a couple of days.

If you want to see the power of a well-designed book page, look at the experience you had with mine. You probably browsed through several book descriptions on the subject of Kindle marketing but somehow mine stood out, and you probably didn't know why at first. Let's do an exercise right now. I want you to click on my biggest competitor and look at his book description page:

How I Sold 1 Million eBooks In 5 Months!
http://amzn.to/NdRAPY

Now, look at mine:

Make A Killing On Kindle
http://amzn.to/N52RSC

Notice the difference? Which one looks more professional? Which one communicates more value? With the Amazon Orange headline, the bolded sentences, italicized words, the standout colors, ordered lists and photos, my book description page telegraphs three powerful, subconscious ideas:

1. **This book must be important.** You rarely or infrequently see formatted book pages, and they're almost always best sellers from popular, respected authors. It's easy to make that premium association to my book.

2. **There's a high likelihood of great content.** Just like a high-quality cover signals high-quality writing, a well-formatted book page indicates superior value.

3. **Amazon endorses this book.** With those Amazon-orange headlines it looks as if Amazon created the page. And you know, they probably reserve that kind of design for books that deserve attention.

Amazon Doesn't Want You To See What I'm About To Show You.
Before you learn how to make your book description pop off the page, you should know something: Amazon doesn't want you to use HTML code. They won't stop you from using it, but they won't help you either. Try searching their help section for "HTML in Book Description." You'll have better luck finding Nemo.

You can also try searching forums and blogs that specialize in Kindle publishing and marketing. Let me know how that works out. You won't see word one on the subject. So the question becomes, if a well-formatted book page moves product, why doesn't Amazon promote the use of HTML code?

Two words: Quality control. Even simple HTML coding can go horribly wrong and make the page look like a landfill. If enough authors made those kinds of mistakes they could seriously tarnish Amazon's brand. By making it impossible for anyone but the most knowledgeable programmers to figure out how to use HTML, Amazon protects the look of their pages.

So, how did I crack the code, given that I only know the most basic HTML? That's a secret I'll take to my shallow, unmarked grave.

The good news is that while discovering how to use HTML is very difficult, using it is not. It's actually quite easy. And with the way I've set up the instructions you can literally copy/paste your way to a wonderfully formatted page.

Still, while you can copy/paste away, you have to check your work arduously because even the tiniest mistake can result in epic ugliness. And because there is no "preview window" to see how it looks before you publish it, you won't find out about any mistakes for up to 24 hours (Amazon takes its sweet time in processing changes to your book page).

This means you run the risk of having hundreds if not thousands of people looking at a badly mangled book page before you have a chance to fix it. Given these facts, you might want to consider hiring an HTML coder to do it for you. It would take them about half an hour. At $35-$70 an hour (the going rate for decent coders) it might be a worthwhile investment.

If you do end up hiring a coder you should learn the basic techniques here anyway because you'll probably want to change your book page as time goes on and it can be a pain to hire a coder to do 10 minutes worth of work.

One last thing. I HIGHLY recommend that you limit your first attempts at using the HTML code to the last paragraph or two of your book page. That way if you make some mistakes you limit the damage. Once you're confident you have it down correctly, then you can move on to coding the rest of the page.

The Secret To HTML Coding On Amazon.

You simply replace the '<' and '>' tags of normal HTML code with "<" and ">" respectively. By the way, "lt" means "less than." "gt" means "greater than."

Let's take the word "something" as an example. Let's italicize it.

Normal HTML: <i>SOMETHING</i>

Amazon HTML: <i>SOMETHING</i>

There are two things I want you to notice:

1. All we've done is replace the '<' and '>' tags with < and >

2. The coding is hard to read. Hence, the possibility of making mistakes is high. So work slowly, carefully and always check your work as soon as Amazon alerts you that your changes were accepted.

Below you will see a chart of the most frequently used HTML codes you would want to use. I'm sure there are more sophisticated uses but you'll find out as I did, that there's such a thing as too much coding. You want your book page to look simple and clean and that argues for less coding not more.

I suggest doing the work on a word processing document (Microsoft Word, Pages or Google Docs) and then copy/pasting the whole thing into Amazon's "Description" text box. Don't do it "live" directly onto the text box because if your internet/wifi service goes out, you will have to reconstruct the entire thing again.

To find the right place to insert the HTML coding follow this path:

1. Sign in to your admin page.
2. Click on your book title.
3. In the section called, "Enter Your Book Details" there's a text box called "Description:" Insert the HTML code here.

Remember, you don't want to "code" or format the entire page with HTML until you've played with it a bit in the last paragraph or two of your description. You WILL make mistakes early on. Better to do them discretely than to ruin your page and have to wait 24 hours to fix it.

Here are the specs for the most common formatting:

BOLD
<b>SOMETHING</b>

Appears in your book page as **SOMETHING**

ITALICS
<i>SOMETHING</i>

Appears in your book page as *SOMETHING*

CENTERED
<center>SOMETHING</center>

Appears centered in your book page as SOMETHING

CENTERED & BOLD
<center> <b>SOMETHING</center></b>

Appears centered in your book page as **SOMETHING**

CENTERED & ITALIC
<center><i>SOMETHING</center></i>

Appears centered in your book page as *SOMETHING*

UNDERLINED
<u>SOMETHING</u>

Appears in your book page as <u>SOMETHING</u>

BULLETED LIST:
<ul>
<li>SOMETHING 1</li>

<li>SOMETHING 2</li>
<li>SOMETHING 3</li>
</ul>

Appears in your book page as:

- SOMETHING
- SOMETHING
- SOMETHING

NUMBERED LIST:
<ol>
<li>SOMETHING 1</li>
<li>SOMETHING 2</li>
<li>SOMETHING 3</li>
</ol>

Appears in your book page as:

1. SOMETHING
2. SOMETHING
3. SOMETHING

H1 HEADLINE:
<h1>SOMETHING</h1>

Appears as the largest font size Amazon allows

H2 Headline (comes out as Amazon orange)
<h2>SOMETHING</h2>

Appears as the second largest font size Amazon allows (in company orange)

H3, H4, H5, H6 formats
(follow same pattern as above)

HEADLINE & CENTERED
<center><h1>SOMETHING</h1> </center>

Appears centered in your book page as SOMETHING. Remember, H1 is the largest font size and that H2 comes out as Amazon orange.

ADDING PICTURES

Amazon does not allow you to upload images. You first have to upload the image to your website and then use its URL link. The following code automatically wraps copy to the right of the image:

<img src="THE URL OF YOUR PIC HERE" align="left" />

Note: Simply paste the URL of your image where indicated, but be sure to keep the quotation marks intact.

ADDING COLOR

Red
<span style="color: #ff0000;">SOMETHING</span>

Cyan
<span style="color: #00FFFF;"> SOMETHING</span>

Blue
<span style="color: #0000FF;"> SOMETHING</span>

Light Blue
<span style="color: #ADD8E6;"> SOMETHING</span>

Purple
<span style="color: #800080;"> SOMETHING</span>

Yellow
<span style="color: #FFFF00;"> SOMETHING</span>

Lime
<span style="color: #00FF00;"> SOMETHING</span>

Fuchsia
<span style="color: #FF00FF;"> SOMETHING</span>

End Notes

1. Amazon might not accept the HTML code if your computer uses curly quotes. The quotes need to be straight. If your word processor curls them automatically, you need to turn off that function. Type in "change quotation mark format" in your word processing software for instructions on how to do it.

2. Some of the HTML examples shown here do not produce the desired effect on the Kindle for iPad app.

CHAPTER TEN

How To Use Amazon's "Look Inside!" Feature To Clinch The Sale.

Amazon gives potential buyers a sneak peak at their books through their "Look Inside!" feature. Browsers get to sample the first 10% of your book. Amazon also has a "Sample sending" feature that sends the first 10% of the book to the customer's gadget of choice—Kindle, iPad, direct-to-computer, etc. This is a fantastic opportunity to close the sale, and I might add, alarmingly, your last. Think about the customer's process so far:

1. They liked the cover and/or title well enough to click on it.
2. Your book description enticed but didn't fully convince.
3. The price may or may not be acceptable.
4. They're near the precipice but they can't commit. Oh, wait! There's the "Look Inside" Feature. They click and read.
5. They decide Yes or No.

Now, the truth is that buying decisions are a bit more complex, but one thing's for sure—if you don't impress them with the first 10% of your book your ROI is DOA.

Front Matter Faux Pas.
The best way to get the "Look Inside" feature to clinch the sale is to make sure readers get to your writing right away. Too many authors fill up the first 10% sampling with useless information like Library of Congress data, dedications, foreword, list of previous books, acknowledgements and other "front matter" that do nothing to sell books.

If I pick up a printed book at a Barnes & Noble and see a lot front matter, I can simply skip to any part of the book I want. Not with Kindle. You can't skim; you can only click from one sequential page to another. Potential buyers have no idea if the next click is going to take them to your writing or to more useless information. This is a recipe for lost sales.

For simplicity's sake, let's say your book is 100 pages long. That means book browsers can sample the first ten pages. You can't impress a customer with your writing if six or seven of those pages are eaten up by "front matter."

Even if your book is two or three hundred pages (and therefore have 20 or 30 pages for the customers to read) it is NEVER a good idea to make a customer click six, seven or more times to get to the meat of what they're looking for. Book sales, in great part, are impulse buys. Every click that doesn't get to your writing is a lost sale.

Let me repeat that: *Every click that doesn't get to your writing is a lost sale.*

There's a reason why Amazon came up with their brilliant "Buy Now With 1-Click" feature. They know that every click on the way to the buy button is an opportunity for buyers to change their minds. They know that their "Shopping Cart Abandonment Rate" is about 70% (proven by industry studies). That means 70% of customers who show serious buying intent--customers who click all the way through a shopping cart--abandon the process at the last minute. If that wrench doesn't tighten your nuts I don't know what will. You MUST make sure that your customers are...

A Click Away From Your Writing.
Once a potential customer hits the "Look Inside" feature they should immediately be taken to your writing. For nonfiction, this should be the Table Of Contents or Introduction. For fiction, it should be the first page of Chapter One or maybe a Cast Of Characters so readers can get a better sense of who inhabits your story lines.

Special note to nonfiction authors: Whether you start with a table of contents or an introduction, you must make sure the information you convey is crystal clear and compelling. Particularly, the table of contents. It is one of the best ways of persuading undecided readers. How many times have you picked up a book at a bookstore and used the table of contents to help you decide if the book's worth buying? It's important that your chapter headings be as specific as possible.

Example of a vague chapter heading:

How To Set Up Your Blog.

Example of a specific chapter heading:

Which Platform Is Best For Your Blog—Wordpress or Blogspot?

How To Tell If Your "Look Inside" Sample Will Help Or Hurt The Sale.
If your book is already published in Kindle, click the Look Inside feature and answer the following questions honestly:

"If I were a complete stranger who didn't know me or my work, would I buy this book based on what I'm reading in the sampler?"

"Does it tell me enough about the book to make me plunk down cold hard cash?"

"Does it give me a good sense of the characters (for fiction) or the subject matter (nonfiction)?"

"Does it move me emotionally?" (fiction)

"Does it offer a solution to my problem?" (nonfiction)

"Do I have a good sense of the characters and plot line?" (fiction)

"Does the book's layout make sense? (Nonfiction)

"Do I want to read more?"

If you can't answer these questions in the affirmative, you need to change the first 10% of your book, even if you have to incur extra formatting costs.

How I Came Up With My 'Look Inside' Feature.
I fretted so much about the Look Inside section for this book, I swear I made my coffee nervous. I knew it would make all the difference in the world if I could get book browsers to sample my writing but I struggled to figure out the most impactful layout. Business books like mine typically start with a table of contents. The problem was that my table of contents looked a bit overwhelming (I purposefully made it a lot longer than the competition). Overwhelm is not a good strategy for selling books, so I did something a little bit out of the usual: I altered the typical sequence of a book sample by putting the Introduction ahead of the table of contents and adding a section called, "Why You Need To Read This Book."

I did this for a couple of reasons. First, several writer friends commented that my table of contents, while comprehensive, was hard to look at. Second, many said they were moved by the honesty with which I described my struggles as a writer in the Introduction. "I would be much more likely to read your table of contents if I knew that you suffered as much I did as a writer," one friend said. So I moved things around and it ended up making a big impact.

The point here is that you should play around with new ways of presenting your writing in the Look Inside section. Talk to friends and ask their opinion. Just know that whatever presentation you decide on for the Look Inside will also appear on the book once it's bought. It's not like you can upload one file for Look Inside and another for the manuscript. I admit my book looks a little cock-eyed to people once they start reading it. Typically, you'd start with a table of contents but mine doesn't appear until page eight.

Where Will You Put The Front Matter?
My advice is to use some combination of the following:

1. Eliminate as much front matter material as you can. Do you really need a dedication or an acknowledgement page? I suspect most people don't, so get rid of them.

2. Combine as much front matter as you can into a page or two (title page, copyright notice, disclaimers, acknowledgment, etc.)

3. After eliminating and combining, put the front matter in the back of the book.

CONVERT: MAKING THE ACTUAL SALE.

CHAPTER ELEVEN

Pricing Strategies.

Seen on a bakery truck...Cakes: 66 cents. Upside down cakes: 99 cents.

If you're committed to making serious coin off your books, you should have one and only one pricing goal: The price that gets you the most amount of revenue.

There are three ways to reach your goal: Test, test and test some more. Getting to your pricing sweet spot starts with a well-thought-out launch price. No matter which of the five launch options you choose below, make sure you don't change any aspect of your book launch for at least four weeks, especially the price. It takes time for Amazon's search engine to index your book. If your sales aren't where you'd like, make sure people can actually find you in the search engine before you start tinkering with the price. Keep track of how well you're doing by inputting keyword phrases into the search box and noting what page of the search results you show up in. Do this every couple of days. Some of my books took more than six weeks to land on page one. *Don't change the price until you consistently show up on at least page two for most of your keyword phrases.* At that point, you'll know that book buyers can find you and you can start playing with different price points.

Launch Option #1 Rock Bottom Pricing (or "The Sofa Change" strategy).
Launching your book at 99 cents may be a good way for you to quickly rise to a top 10 or 20 ranking. The operative word here is "may." There is no "will" on Amazon. You won't know until you test it. Ninety-nine cents has been an effective launch strategy for some of my books and a disaster for others.

Rock bottom pricing means you're not going to make much money, even if you hit a top 10 category, so keep in mind a 99 cent pricing should be a launch strategy, not an ongoing one.

Here are the reasons why 99 cents may work as a launching point:

- There's almost no "barrier to entry" for customers.
- It's a total impulse buy with so little risk it isn't worth mentioning.

- It promotes sampling of new authors.
- It may build a base of fans willing to pay more for your other books.
- It may help rank you in the top 10 or 20 in your category.
- It may help you appear in the "Customers who bought this item..." list of more popular books.

And here are the reasons it may not:

- There's a sizable part of the market that equates such a low price with crap. Take me, for example. Or rather, my mentality. I've never bought a 99-cent book. Never will. Anybody who has bought a decent amount of books knows what I do: If the chances of buying an unsatisfying book at $9.99 run high, what are the chances with a 99 cent book? Stratospheric.

By the way, most 99-cent books fail either at a launch or maintenance price. Try this: Search Kindle for fiction or non-fiction books, sorted by lowest price first. Many of those books rank so low they literally don't have a ranking!

- Once you've trained somebody to buy your work at .99 cents they expect your other work to be that cheap. Because the low price devalued your work, some people may feel that you're ripping them off at $4.99 for your next book.

- At .99 cents, did they buy your book because of the content or because they couldn't pass up a bargain? Many will have done it as a bargain and never get around to actually reading your work (trust me, if they bought yours at .99 they bought a LOT of other books for that price or close to it).

- There's very little loyalty at 99 cents. The decision point isn't quality; it's price. And that means you're going to die by the same sword that cut you that first slice of life.

The Problem With Rock Bottom Pricing.
I know I'm going on like a wounded cat about the pitfalls of a low-ball pricing strategy, but allow me a quick story. A woman is walking down the street and sees this magnificent Parrott in the window of the pet shop for only fifty dollars. She goes into the shop and asks the owner why he would sell such a superb bird for that little? The pet shopkeeper explains that the parrot is a little rough around the edges having come from a house of ill repute. The woman says that she doesn't care—she just can't pass up that price.

She takes the bird home and takes the cage into the living room. She removes the cage cover and the bird looks around and says: "New House, New Madam." The woman thinks, "Well, if that's what the owner meant by rough I got a great deal." Her daughters come over that weekend to see the parrot. They walk into the living room and the parrot looks around and says:" New House, New Madam and New Hotties." The woman beams. Then her husband walks in and the parrot says, "Hi, Robert."

My point, and I do have one, is that a magnificently low price usually means a magnificent flaw comes with it. Offer 25% off a loaf of bread and shoppers will think they got a bargain. Offer 75% off and they'll think there's something wrong with it.

It's one thing to use rock bottom pricing to launch; quite another for it to be your business model.

Launch Option # 2 Pricing To Your Profile.
According to a major analysis of Kindle ebooks by www.ebookfriendly.com, the average price of a self-published book is $1.40. Obviously, there are many priced free and many priced at $9.99 or more. But the average is $1.40. That's really low. You may want to start off by pricing your book according to the profile you best fit. I don't just mean looking at what other books in your genre are charging. That's just the starting point. By pricing to your profile I mean comparing the totality of your enterprise to the totality of your competitors'. That includes the genre, your platform (any built-in audience you may have from previous works), the content quality, the number of books you've authored, market size, reader passion/need for the subject matter you're writing about, perceived value and book length. These are very important factors. It's unrealistic to think that your 50-page book as a first time self-published author without a fan base should be priced similar to a 200-page book by an established author with a legacy publisher, even though it's a similar subject matter.

To "price to profile," pick out the books that most closely resemble yours in:

- **Backlist Or Series.**
If you have a backlist (for newbies, that means previously published books) or a series, you'd want to compare yourself to other authors with a similar profile. Anybody with a backlist or series has more flexibility with launch prices because there's an echo effect to sales. For example, people that buy one of my dating books often buy my other ones.

- **Publishing Arm (published or self-published).**
Are you a self-published author pricing yourself to a similar author signed by Simon & Schuster? Probably not a good idea. Big legacy publishers cut marketing deals with Amazon for special placement and promotions. You may actually be a better writer but the marketing tilt is against you.

- **Book length.**
Amazon publishes your page count at the top of the book description section. Unless you're writing some kind of esoteric technical manual or writing about

a subject rarely covered, there is little possibility that you can charge "full price" for a much shorter book. Price accordingly. And don't forget, buyers can return ebooks for a full refund within seven days. If you sell a 30-page book for $9.99 you're going to have unacceptably high returns.

• **Content quality.**
This takes a realistic assessment of your writing powers vs. competitors in your genre. For example, I think I'm above average in my field (sex, dating and relationships). I'm no Dan Savage but the quality of my writing is superior compared to most of my competitors. On the other hand, when I write books that are not in my main field, I don't actually feel like I'm "above average" so I'm more likely to start my pricing lower.

• **Field Density.**
How crowded is the field you're writing in? The more competitors you have the more "commodity pricing" you may have to adopt.

• **Market Size & Reader Passion.**
How big is the market for your book? Big markets usually mean lots of competitors which means commodity pricing. Along with market size, reader passion is a big driver. If you're in a new, rising market like the supernatural/paranormal/werewolves and vampire genre a few years ago, your pricing would be very different than it would be now when the market is glutted.

• **Perceived Value.**
Are you writing about something few authors have touched? What will the reader get from this book above and beyond what they paid for it? Is there a perception that an investment in your book will pay off in a bigger way than other books? If so, you're in a position to charge more.

The biggest advantage to "pricing to your profile" is that potential buyers won't balk at the price. You'll be perceived as charging a market rate for your book.

Launch Option #3 Top of the line pricing.
That means $9.99. Anything more and Amazon lowers your royalty to 35%. I have started a couple of my books at $9.99, worked my way down and found that they actually worked best at the highest price! I'm glad that I started out high because it meant I was earning money all through my price testing (this is not necessarily true if you start at .99 cents). The biggest benefit of starting high is that if you guess right (all launch prices are educated guesses) you won't have lost income.

Launch Option #4 $2.99 Fiction Or $4.99 For Nonfiction.
From observation, data analysis, my own experience and that of my clients, a pricing norm is beginning to emerge among self-published authors: $2.99

for fiction and $4.99 for nonfiction. It's not a bad idea to start here if the other options seem too scary or confusing.

Non-fiction books command higher prices than fiction books. This is mostly due to perceived value. People are willing to pay more for something that solves their problem than something that entertains them for a few hours. A book that can have an impact on your finances or love life is perceived as more valuable than a book that helps you escape reality for a short while, and therefore you're willing to pay more for it.

Most people never underline passages or pick up a fiction book again once they've read it. People often highlight nonfiction books and revisit them again and again as a reference. To understand the profound pricing difference between fiction and nonfiction books, consider the analysis I did at the time of this writing: The Top 10 Nonfiction Full-Length Kindle Ebooks averaged $10.35 while the Top 10 Fiction Ebooks averaged $6.29. That's a whopping 39% difference.

Launch Option #5 A Little Bit Higher Or Lower Than Options 1-4.
This approach is simple. Decide which of the price points in the first four options you like best and go slightly higher or lower. Let's say you decided on $2.99 from option #4. You can go lower ($1.99) or higher ($3.99). Remember, setting a launch price is an art form, an educated guess. And you shouldn't fret too much about making the right decision because as you'll soon see, you're going to change it soon anyway.

How To Increase Or Decrease Your Post-Launch Prices.
Once you start showing up on page one or two of the search results for your keyword phrases (about two to six weeks) it'll be time for a price increase (or decrease, depending on what price you started at). Remember, the goal here isn't to maximize the price point; it's to increase overall revenue. What we are testing is not the price point per se, but the revenue it brings in. All of us would be more comfortable with a $9.99 tag on our books because full pricing validates our work. But what if you could make more money at $2.99 because the volume is so much higher? Testing is the only way you're going to find out. Here are some best practice templates to get you going:

Escalating The Price When You Launch At 99 Cents.

Step 1: *Submit the price at .99.*

Step 2: *Wait 24 hours for Amazon to process.*

Step 3: *Wait until your book shows up on page one or two of the search engine results for your keyword phrases (about 2 to 6 weeks).*

Keep track of sales through a spreadsheet. Track the daily ranking so you can make an association between your ranking and units sold. It'll come in handy as a shorthand to your sales without having to log in to your admin section (for example, if you see a ranking near 30,000 you know you've sold about three books). For consistency, input the rankings and units sold into the spreadsheet every 24 hours (I do mine at about the same time every morning).

Let's say you've been selling briskly at 99 cents. How do you know if you should escalate the price to see if you can get more revenue? You don't and that's why you should raise the price. Right now, you're trying to establish the best range of monthly revenue for your book. You may be making a lot of money now but who's to say you wouldn't double it if you charged more? The proof of the pudding is always in the eating. So let's eat!

Step 5: Price Increase (To $1.99).
Keep it at $1.99 for two weeks, unless you see a dramatic reduction in revenue early on. But I seriously doubt that's going to happen.

Step 6: Price Increase (to $2.99).
Assuming you make more at $1.99 than at .99 cents, raise it to $2.99 for two weeks. Again, the only time you want to cut it short is when you experience a dramatic drop-off in revenue after about two weeks. I seriously doubt that will happen because until now you've been operating under a 35% royalty. Amazon changes your royalties to 70% at the $2.99 price point.

Step 7: Keep Escalating The Price By $1.
Rinse, lather, repeat. Keep raising the price by $1 every two weeks. Eventually, you're going to experience the "market price" for your book. This is the price at which you get the most total revenue. This is the point at which lowering or increasing the price lowers total revenue. There is no way to tell where you will end up. Once you've reached a critical mass price point, sit back and let the Amazon Gods do their work. You can rest. Well, until things start falling out of bed and you have to start testing price again (this can happen for a variety of reasons—new competitors come to market, you get bad reviews, etc.).

De-Escalating The Price When You Launch At $9.99.

Step 1: Submit the price at $9.99.

Step 2-4: See above.
Again, you're going to be faced with the same question. How do you know if you should change the price at the end of two weeks? You don't. That's why you should lower it. I'll repeat this again and again: Price doesn't matter; revenue does.

Step 5: Lower the price by $1 or by 50%, depending on the revenue produced.
If you're somewhat pleased by sales, lower the price by $1. If you're alarmed because the book is hardly selling, cut it in half to $4.99. There's no right or wrong here. Use your gut instinct. The reason there is no right or wrong is that whatever price you choose is temporary anyway—you're going to change it in two weeks. Let's say you lowered the price by $1. Wait two weeks. Did you make more or less money? If you made less then raise the price back to $9.99. If you made more, lower the price by another $1. If there's no change, keep lowering it by a $1 every two weeks. You're on a treasure hunt for the price that drives the most revenue.

Escalating The Price When You Launch between .99 cents and $9.99.

Step 1: Submit the price. For this example, let's use $2.99.

Step 2-4: See above.

Now that you've established a baseline for sales at $2.99, do you go up or down at the end of the test period? The question depends on how you stack up on your "Price To Profile" ratio. If others in your profile range tend to have priced their book higher then I'd increase the price by $1. If they priced it lower, then lower it by $1. Again, there is no right answer because you're going to change it in two weeks anyway. Follow this formula until you feel comfortable that you've reached the "market price."

Getting To The Revenue-Maximized Price.
Once you start the price testing process you're going to see that some books have a clear and distinct revenue-maximized price while others do not. You might find it's a moving target. Regardless, testing will give you invaluable insight into how the market moves around your book.

On a closing note, do not freak out when you've determined your revenue-maximized price and start seeing wild swings in sales. It's normal to have fluctuations over time, especially with low numbers. And they will be low. I've never had a book start out of the gate with high sales. It's a slow build. Buy yourself some freak-out protection by monitoring your spreadsheet on a daily basis. Look closely and you'll see deep valleys and high peaks. As long as your weekly average stays solid you have nothing to worry about. The only time you should change the price is when you see the revenue trending downward for several weeks in a row.

70% Royalty Means 66% Take Home Pay.
Amazon trumpets a top royalty rate of 70% but beware the not-so-hidden costs:

1)   Amazon charges a "delivery cost" of about $0.06 per unit sold. It varies by the number of megabytes in your book file. The bigger the book, the bigger the charge.

2)   Amazon takes out taxes in some territories like the United Kingdom.

3)   Even though you may set the royalty rate at 70% for books sold in the U.S., some of those sales will only earn a 35% royalty. Amazon does not explain this clearly in their help section, but KDP support emailed me explaining that any unit sold outside of the "70% territories" listed below gets categorized as a U.S. sale with a 35% royalty rate:

Andorra
Austria
Belgium
Canada
France
Germany
Italy
Liechtenstein
Luxembourg
Monaco
San Marino
Switzerland
Spain
United Kingdom (including Guernsey, Jersey and Isle of Man)
United States
Vatican City

Let's say that somebody living in Mexico, which is outside of the above territories, buys your book. Even though you pegged the royalty rate at 70%, the Mexican sale will be coded as a U.S. sale under a 35% royalty rate. It's impossible to project how many of the books tagged with a 70% royalty rate will only get 35%, but it will be enough to lower your total take by one or two percentage points.

Between Amazon's delivery costs, taxes and sales outside the 70% royalty territories, my net revenue translates to an effective take-home pay of 66%. A loss of four percentage points is a big deal. As a cost of doing business, it's more than what PayPal or credit cards charge retailers. Do yourself a favor and project your income using a 66% take-home pay versus a 70% royalty. It'll be a lot closer to the truth.

CHAPTER TWELVE

Getting Reviews That Make People Want To Buy Your Book.

A few years ago, Yale professors Judith A. Chevalier and Dina Mayzlin did a study on the effect of user-generated Amazon reviews on sales. The authors made some fascinating observations:

1. Good reviews significantly increase book sales.
2. 1-star reviews have a greater power to depress sales than 5-star reviews have to increase them.
3. Reviews are overwhelmingly positive at both Amazon and Barnes & Noble.
4. There are far more reviews on Amazon than Barnes & Noble, and they tend to have a much higher word count.

Just how much of an impact can good reviews make? While this is very hard to gage, the authors make a theoretical case:

Consider a book with no reviews at either site [Amazon and Barnes & Noble] whose price and other characteristics would suggest a sales rank of 500 at both sites. The posting of an additional 3 reviews at Amazon.com, if it didn't alter the sales rank at BN.com, would be expected to lower the sales rank to number 327, implying incremental sales of approximately 57 books per week.

One of the more fascinating aspects of the study was the discovery of how powerful a 1-star review has to decimate sales. In fact, it has more power to lower sales than a 5-star does to increase them. This brought an eyebrow-raising observation from the authors:

One could argue that posting 1 star reviews of competing books could be a reasonable strategy for an author. We acknowledge that this may be true, although it is not at all clear that two books on the same subject, for example, are substitutes rather than complements.

For the record, I think it would be hideous for any author to do that.

The Difference Between Amazon and BN.com.
The Yale study found some fascinating differences between the two sites:

- BN.com's total sales equal about 15% of Amazon.com's North American sales.
- BN.com has way more books with zero reviews than Amazon (54.22% versus 12.61%).

How Many People Actually Post A Review?
Now that we have hard evidence of what most of us know intuitively (reviews affect sales), it becomes abundantly clear that you must do everything you can to get reviews posted to your books. The problem is that most people who love your book will not write one. Think of your own behavior. When was the last time you read a book, returned to Amazon, searched for it, clicked on the title and wrote a review?

To show you just how few people do it, consider this example. According to Amazon, the most reviewed book on the site is Harry Potter And The Order Of The Phoenix with almost 6,000 reviews. Amazing, no? Not really. Not when you realize Amazon sold millions and millions of copies!

My back of the envelope math shows that .0002% of readers of one of the best selling books of all time posted a review. In their blog, Freakonomics authors Steven Levitt and Stephen Dubner, estimate that 1 in 1,000 book purchasers post a review on Amazon. That's .001%.

My point, and I do have one, is two-fold:
1. Reviews are hard to come by.
2. They make a HUGE difference in your sales.

The good news is that you don't have to have a lot of reviews for your book to sell well. I know some best sellers that have just a handful of reviews. But the challenge is there and we must meet it: How do we get good reviews posted to our book page? We can do this by...

Using Permission-Based Strategies.
Ever see an empty tip jar when you're settling your bill at the cash register? Studies show that you're far less likely to leave a tip in an empty jar than one that already has money in it. That's the concept of "social proof" at work—we use other people's cues to guide our behavior. It's the reason empty clubs make people wait outside. It's social proof to people driving by that this is the place to party.

For our purposes, book reviews are social proof. Consider two competing books: They cost the same and cover the same subject matter. They both have clever titles, a well-designed cover and a compelling book description. But one has fifteen reviews and the other has none. Which is the better book? Social proof says most of us will pick the one with all the reviews. In the absence of other evidence, those reviews are "proof" the book is better.

Obviously, the more reviews you get, the stronger the social proof. Luckily, you don't need THAT many reviews to get your sales going. In fact, you don't need many at all. At the time of this writing, the sixth best selling book on Kindle was All About Steve: The Story of Steve Jobs and Apple from the Pages of Fortune. It has seven reviews. I have an ebook that hit the #1 spot in the Sex category. It generates thousands and thousands of dollars every month. It has six reviews.

My point is that more is better, but a few is fine. Now, let's go back to the tip jar analogy. Ask the baristas at Starbucks—an empty tip jar is negative social proof. If they want more tips they have to slide a little positive social proof into it. A book page without reviews displays negative social proof. If you want more reviews—and sales—you need to social proof it. You do it by...

Placing 'Starter' Reviews.

By this, I mean having you, your family, your friends or a hired gun submit the kind of reviews outlined below. I understand that some authors may feel uncomfortable doing this, but I personally don't see the difference between posting a few reviews into your empty book page and putting a few bucks into the empty tip jar. Both give permission for people to take action. The good news is that you only need six 'starter' reviews to make an impact. Here's why: Amazon displays the three "Most Helpful" reviews in full on the left side of the page and the ten Most Recent reviews on the right—a total of thirteen reviews can appear on your page. But six is all you need (three on the left, three on the right). It fills the page out nicely and gives ample social proof this is not only a book worth buying but worth writing a review if you do.

The goal here is to provide honest reviews of your book, warts and all. The worst thing you can do is fill them with so many ass kissing adjectives that your lips are set to a permanent pucker. What you want are helpful reviews, insightful explorations that give people a better understanding so they can make an informed decision. Here are the steps to an artful presentation of reviews:

1. Make Sure The Reviewers Actually Buy Your Book.

I leave it up to you to decide whether you should do this yourself (open six different Amazon accounts), or get your friends, family or copywriters to do it. Either way, they should purchase the book to get the preferred "Amazon Verified Purchase" label. This gives reviews credibility. I can tell you this for a fact: Most reviews that don't have the "Verified Purchase" label were planted by the author or his surrogates.

2. Make Sure The Critiques Read Like A True Book Review.

Judge on merit, be helpful, shed light. A well thought-out review contains the following:

1. Brief Synopsis.
2. The basic themes of the book.
3. A judgment on writing style.
4. A recommendation of who should read the book.
5. Articulate how it made you feel and what it made you think.
6. A summary of what happened and what it meant (without any spoilers).
7. What you loved or hated and why.
8. How well did the book achieved its goal.
9. Whether you would recommend it to others and why.

As stated before, your goal is to create six starter reviews. There is a very particular formula I want you to follow:

The First Review: A Five-Star "Main Review" That Your Friends Can Vote "Most Helpful."

You want this to be the review every browser sees first. Forever. No matter how many other reviews you get. How do you keep this main review from being pushed off the page as future reviews come in? You're going to ask all your friends to scroll down to the bottom of the review where they will click the YES button on the question, "Was this review helpful to you?" Amazon will put it—and keep it—at the top of their "Most Helpful Customer Reviews" section (as long as it doesn't get outvoted as most helpful).

This main review is crucial to your strategy because it will be the first (and maybe the only) review browsers are likely to read. For that reason, it's imperative that it gives an honest, comprehensive critique. Here's an example from Managing The Stress Of Infertility:

> Despite A Few Flaws, A Must Read For All Women In Treatment For Infertility.
>
> I bought this book because I saw the author on TV. As somebody who cried every other day because I couldn't get pregnant, her advice comforted me greatly. I'm happy to report that her book was as good as her interview. It gave me new ways to cope with the emotional roller coaster I was on. While there are a few missing pieces in the book, it's a must-read for any woman who's having a hard time coping emotionally with the stress of infertility treatment.

THE GOOD

• The tone is pitch-perfect. Warm and compassionate, just as you'd expect from an infertility counselor (apparently the author had herself undergone infertility treatment, which made her advice all the more helpful).

• She addresses every situation that causes stress and despair and shows you how to either avoid, manage or resolve them. For example, she tells you what to say in uncomfortable social situations (like somebody asking how many children you have).

• Throughout each chapter there are personal stories from the author's infertility clients. Reading these stories made me feel like I had just joined an instant support group—that I wasn't alone, that my feelings were normal and shared by others, and that there are real, practical solutions to the typical stressors of being in treatment.

• Surprisingly, there's a section on breath work. At first, I thought it was a waste but she has a convincing argument that breathing patterns are the most powerful resource for changing our emotional state. She walks you through specific breath patterns to either calm or energize you. They're easy to follow and the results are almost immediate. It's possibly the best section in the book.

THE BAD

• The author doesn't address the medical aspects of infertility. For example, I have polycystic ovaries (PCOS). I would have liked to see more information on specific medical issues like that.

• The book is fairly short. Given that she's a yoga teacher herself, I was surprised the author didn't have an entire chapter, with pictures, on yoga poses for fertility.

• While the chapter on sexual passion and pleasure was more thorough than other infertility books I've read, it still didn't answer many of the questions I had.

Despite these drawbacks, I highly recommend this book. First, because it's the only book devoted entirely to managing the stress of infertility (as opposed to all the other books that emphasize medical treatment, diet regimens, or first person accounts). If you're feeling emotionally overwhelmed by the struggles of conceiving, you should buy this book.

The trick to writing a believable, warts-and-all review without damaging your sales prospects is to highlight negatives that don't mean much to the buyer. In the above example, the book is criticized for shortchanging the sexual passion chapter. Fine. Almost nobody is going to buy this book for sexual instruction. But bringing a negative up, no matter how small, increases the credibility of the review.

The Second & Third Review: Solid To Stellar Critiques.
They should be nearly as comprehensive as the "Main Review." You will also have your friends (as well as yourself through your different accounts) mark it as a "helpful" review. Remember, Amazon chooses the three "Most Helpful Reviews" at the top left of the review section and prints them in full. They cut off the reviews on the right after four sentences with a "Read More" link. Don't take the chance that a bad review somehow floats to the top. Buy yourself a little insurance (at least temporarily) and vote your reviews "Most Helpful." Give your second and third reviews four and five stars.

The Fourth Review: A Three-Star 'Middlin' Critique.
Just like nobody in a coffee shop is going to believe a tip jar stuffed with hundred dollar bills, nobody is going to believe a series of five-star, ass kissing reviews. If the first reviews are a couple of dollar bills in the tip jar, then this review should be the nickels and dimes. It should be a three-star critique that shows a bit of disappointment. Those aren't hard to write. As an author I can tell you exactly where the weak points of my books are.

Here's a great example from one of my dating books:

> Useful Information; Confusing Structure.
>
> Though the book is fairly packed with useful advice, it's undermined by a structure that sometimes makes it difficult to follow. For example, the chapters themselves are thorough, concise and helpful, but they do not flow easily from one to the other. They don't build on each other. That is a shame because the information in this book would help anybody who wants to improve their online dating chances. While I would recommend this book to entrepreneurs, I'd just as strongly recommend a new editor for the author.

The Fourth, Fifth & Sixth Reviews.
These should be a mix of four and five star reviews. In the end, you want Amazon to average out your reviews to about four and half stars. Again, make sure the critiques are thoughtful, insightful and helpful. Do NOT have them sound like a cheerleading squad watching their team come from behind.

Should You Pump Up The Number Of Reviews As High As You Can?
This would require getting just about every friend or acquaintance to do a short review. To be honest, I'm of a mixed mind on this one. On the one hand, the more reviews you have the more "social proof" you get. On the other hand, those friends and family are almost guaranteed to write the kind of obviously planted reviews that sound like they came from people who owed you a favor. And once a book browser gets a whiff of that it can really hurt your conversion rate.

As I stated previously, more is better but few are fine. If you can get friends and acquaintances to actually say something insightful and meaningful about the book (ha!) I say go for it. If not, six is all you need.

Getting Good Reviews By Leveraging Kindle's 'Before You Go' Feature.
Recently, Amazon introduced a feature called "Before You Go" in its Kindle e-reader. The last page of every book is now a screen prompting readers to rate the book on a scale of 1 to 5 stars and share their feelings about it on Facebook and Twitter. This is another characteristically brilliant maneuver on Amazon's part. The best time to get people to review or share on social media is right after they finish a book while emotions are running high, and now they've developed a way to do that.

The Before You Go feature will be a good friend if it generates four and five-starred reviews for your book and a mortal enemy if it doesn't. Which is why I told you at the start of this book that I can only help you if you're a good writer with a worthy book and a thirsty market. If you've got a lousy book, the Before You Go feature has the potential to ruin your sales (which is a good thing. You shouldn't be publishing lousy books in the first place!).

It's Free Social Media Publicity For Your Book.
If you've got a great book, the Before You Go feature has the potential to strap a rocket to the back of your sales. Again, by hotwiring itself to Facebook, Kindle gives its readers the ability to update their status with a short message about your book. But that isn't all. Kindle automatically attaches a color image of your cover with a link to your book page!

Think about it. Buyers of your book can tell all their friends they loved it and invite them to check it out by clicking on an attached link. The feature also works on Twitter. Readers can say something about your book and Kindle attaches a link to its page. That, my friends, is remarkable. It is a brilliant word-of-mouth system that could ripple out to hundreds, thousands, even millions of people. There's an old saying in marketing: "Advertising you pay for, publicity you pray for." The Before You Go feature is The Lord's Prayer, the Twenty-Third Psalm, and The Hail Mary all rolled into one.

The Most Important Thing You Can Do To Get Readers To Promote Your Book On Facebook And Twitter.
Just because Kindle gives readers an opportunity to share their feelings about your book on Facebook and Twitter, it doesn't mean they will. First, the quality of your writing has to inspire so much passion that it motivates people to share it. People are not going to tell the world they just spent three hours reading a mediocre book.

Second, depending on how you've formatted your book, they might not ever get to the Before You Go feature. Let me explain. Before You Go is the last page of your book. If you follow the end of your novel or how-to with back matter like an index, bibliography, etc., there's a great chance readers will simply turn their Kindles off before they get to the Before You Go feature. Think of it this way—there is a gap between the end of your book and the beginning of the Before You Go screen. The bigger the gap, the less likely you'll get a starred rating or a Facebook/Twitter share.

Take Elmore Leonard's novel Djobouti as an example of what not to do (thanks to Steve Lewis, author of In-Book Promotion: Using the Kindle's Built-In Features to Increase Sales for the example). There are about 10 screens between the end of the book and the Before You Go. They're filled with clutter and advertising. After you finish reading the last sentence of his novel you have to click through ten pages before the Before You Go feature pops up. Now, I ask you, how many people are going to click through all those pages? Very few. And that's a shame, because Elmore Leonard could have a huge, FREE social media word-of-mouth campaign if his publisher were a little smarter about how they laid out the book. It is therefore with the most blinding glimpse of the obvious that I present to you the most effective thing you can do to encourage Facebook and Twitter sharing:

Limit the number of pages that appear after your writing ends.

In the best of all possible worlds, you'd want the Before You Go feature to pop up immediately after The End. But the truth is, you have to balance competing interests. After all, the perfect place to sell your other books and services is right after your book ends. Only you can decide what should have precedence—an increased chance for a review/social media share or an increased chance for after-market sales. Either way, there are two pages that I strongly recommend you put right after The End...

1. An engaging author bio that makes people like you enough to buy your other books and/or make a Facebook/Twitter share.
People like to give business to people they like. Now that you've impressed them with your work, keep the love going with a captivating author bio.

That can make a big impact on the reader's next move. They're more likely to post a share or buy another book if they also feel strongly about you personally. The best way to do that is to...

Write a personally engaging bio anchored by a warm and friendly photo. Don't write a resume. Write a story. Make your career an engaging anecdote that mixes the credibility boosters of a resume with the appeal of a well-told story. Anchor it with a picture that makes you look friendly and accessible. Knowing what you look like goes a long way to forging a personal connection. At the end of your bio, readers should be thinking, "Wow, I really like this author. He (she) seems like such a cool person."

This puts the reader in an expansive mood. First, they loved your book, now they love you! I see another purchase in your future. Here is the About The Author section I use in my dating books:

About Michael Alvear.
I was writing the occasional op-ed piece for newspapers like The New York Times, The Los Angeles Times and Newsweek when my career took an unlikely turn. A local editor approached me about writing an irreverent sex advice column. I thought, "Awesome! Send me your cutest employees and I'll get started." I sort of became known as the "East Coast Dan Savage." I went on to write my first book, a collection of sex advice columns, Men Are Pigs But We Love Bacon (Kensington)

That led to a major production company in London asking me if I'd like to audition for a co-hosting role in a sex makeover series called The Sex Inspectors. With the screen test cameras rolling, I remember the production chief asking me what I thought of women faking their orgasms. "That's nothing," I sniffed. "Men fake whole relationships."

I got the job.

The show went on to be an international hit, airing in 12 countries, including the U.S. on HBO. It led to my biggest book yet, Sex Inspectors Master Class: *How To Have An Amazing Sex Life (Penguin)*.

Once during filming, I sat on the bed with a woman I was advising (don't worry, we were fully clothed—it wasn't that kind of show!). The video cameras that we put throughout her house showed how cruelly she rejected her husband's advances. I said, "Put your arm around me, I want to show you how you reject your husband." I whacked her arm away like it was an unwanted fly and looked away from her. Indignantly, she said, "I do NOT do that!" I said, "Yes, you do." She knew I was right. I could see her face softening. I leaned in. "Can I tell you a secret?" She nodded. I cupped my hand around her ear and whispered something. She started bawling. The producer, director and audio people went nuts because the microphone didn't pick up what I said. The director stopped the filming to give the woman time to compose, took me aside and asked, "What the hell did you say to make her cry like that?

I said, "*Men have feelings, too.*"

I love giving advice to people. I love to see barriers crack and humanity come to the surface. I hope I was able to that with the book you're holding in your hands and that you've enjoyed reading it as much as I did writing it.

This author bio sets me up nicely for the next step. First, they had a good experience of me as an author, and now they've had a good experience of me as a person. If I ask them to rate the book and share it through Facebook and Twitter, they are far more likely to do it. Here are two more examples of effective author bios:

From novelist Roni Loren:
Roni wrote her first romance novel at age fifteen when she discovered writing about boys was way easier than actually talking to them. Since then, her flirting skills haven't improved, but she likes to think her storytelling ability has. After earning a master's degree in social work from LSU, she worked in a mental hospital, counseled birthmothers as an adoption coordinator, and did management recruiting in her PJs. But she always returned to writing.

Though she'll forever be a New Orleans girl at heart, she now lives in Dallas with her husband and son. If she's not working on her latest sexy story, you can find her reading, watching reality television, or indulging in her unhealthy addiction to rock concerts.

As you can see here (and in Chapter Thirteen), there are many ways to write an author bio that reveals something important about you. Readers are more likely now to rate or share your book. But don't leave that to chance. The very next page after your author bio should be...

2. A specific request asking readers to review the book or post a share on Facebook or Twitter.
You have the power to get readers to post a review or share. It's the power of the ask. Not any ask, mind you, but a specially crafted one. Let me explain. There is a well-known principle of human behavior that says people are far more likely to grant your request if you give them a reason for it. It doesn't even have to be a compelling reason. It just has to be an explicitly stated reason. In his book, Influence, The Psychology Of Persuasion, psychologist Robert Cialdini describes an experiment showing that the chances of getting people to do what you ask can rise by 30 percentage points if you give any justification for it.

"People simply like to have reasons for what they do," he writes.

How does that apply to what we're doing? You need to give a reason why you're requesting buyers to review or a post a share. Here's an example of how I do it.

One Last Thing...

When you turn the page, Kindle will give you the opportunity to rate the book and share your thoughts on Facebook and Twitter. If you believe the book is worth sharing, would you take a few seconds to let your friends know about it? If it turns out to make a difference in their lives, they'll be forever grateful to you. As I will.

All the best,

Michael Alvear

But What Will You Do With The Back Matter?

Depending on the type of book you're writing, you may need a slew of back matter: Appendix, bibliography, endnotes, glossary, index, etc. Where will you put them? On your website (we finally found a useful thing for your blog!). Just put a link in your manuscript and point it to your website. The Kindle e-reader has a built-in browser. It'll take them directly to the page you designate on your site. Readers who truly care will clink on it. The ones who don't will be taken to the Before You Go screen.

End Notes

Many people are not seeing a "Before You Go" feature on their e-reader device. For instance, it doesn't appear on the Kindle for iPad. However I've seen it on all Kindle devices made on or after 2012. It's possible that Amazon is simply testing the feature on certain devices. For Amazon's explanation on "Before You Go" click here: *http://amzn.to/RclEN1*.

Notes

CHAPTER THIRTEEN

Overcoming "Pre-Buyers Remorse" With The Author's Page in Author Central.

It's common to get "pre-buyer's remorse," that awful feeling you're about to make a purchase you'll later regret. It often stems from a suspicion that you're being bamboozled. After all, if the author's so good, why doesn't he or she have a publisher backing them up? A credibility gap causes the doubt. In the absence of a familiar name, an established publishing house, or reviews by legitimate news outlets, the buyer senses a plausibility deficit.

Amazon's Author Central micro-site is a way of shrinking that deficit. It helps overcome skepticism by providing an author bio, a picture, videos and a feed from your blog (if you have one). This information, properly curated, helps educate customers about who you are, what you do and what you've accomplished.

It's a stand-alone site that reviewers can click to, but more importantly, it automatically places your author bio and photo straight to every one of your book pages. The feed appears in the Reviews section (under More About The Author) with a link to your Author Page.

How To Get Started

Visit www.authorcentral.com to create an account and "claim" your book(s). It's free. The directions are simple and self-evident. Just make sure to confirm the email Amazon sends you as soon as possible. It can take up to 7 days to process your confirmation.

How To Create An Effective Author Page

There are many ways to create a compelling author bio. For example, it doesn't matter if you write it in first person or third. As for length, there's no rule but I do have a guideline: Your author bio should be about the size of the bottom half of a bathing suit—short enough to catch attention but long enough to cover the essentials. There is no one formula, but all great bios do some or all of the following:

- Create an identity.

- Highlight a single defining moment that shaped or inspired a life decision.

- Give insight and perspective without descending into needless details.

- Stick to the facts and avoid hyperbole. Don't discredit yourself with exaggerations.

- Deliver the information concisely.

- Use humor (when possible).

- List awards and accomplishments without bragging.

- State your goals and intentions for the reader.

- Showcase "credibility boosters" -- items that build a strong argument for claimed authority.

- Describe differentiators that make you stand out from the competition.

CHAPTER FOURTEEN

Making Sure Your Book Is An Effective After-Sales Ambassador.

In Chapter Twelve we discussed Kindle's Before You Go feature, which gives readers the opportunity to rate your book and share it on Facebook and Twitter. I outlined the dilemma you will face: Every page you add after the end of your book decreases the chances that the reader will rate or share your book simply because they might stop reading before they get to the Before You Go page.

This is not an issue if you're a one-book fiction author. But if you're a multiple-book author in any genre or a business author with other lines of business the reader might be interested in (consulting, webinars, etc.) you should seriously consider adding a page or two to communicate these opportunities, even if it means decreasing the chances of a rating/share. Readers are most receptive to your message at the end of the book. They've connected to your work and with an engaging author bio, they'll connect to you as a person. The next step is to create a page that merchandises your other work or capabilities. Below you'll see an example of how I do it (explanation to follow):

More Books From Michael Alvear.[1]
The Flirty Text Message Helper: Witty Texts For Clever People.
A collection of witty texts you can send to your crushes. Hand-picked by our team of writers & researchers, there are no cliches, lame poems or cheesy pickup lines. Categorized by 19 dating circumstances, these texts will help you build attraction and score a date.

Click here to check it out on Kindle[2]: http://amzn.to/xjUyYj

Questions For The Author?[3]
Email me at *mike@mikealvear.com*.

Want to be on Mike's Free Monthly Dating Newsletter?
Sign up at www.mikealvear.com.

Need Consulting Advice?
Contact me at mike@mikealvear.com.

One Last Thing...[4]

When you turn the page, Kindle will give you the opportunity to rate the book and share your thoughts through an automatic feed to your Facebook and Twitter accounts. If you believe your friends would get something valuable out of this book, I'd be honored if you'd post your thoughts. And if you feel particularly strong about the contributions this book made to your own love life, I'd be eternally grateful if you posted a review on Amazon. Just click here and it will take you directly to the page [5] : http://amzn.to/N52RSC.

All the best,

Michael

Explanations:

[1] *Write a description of your book(s).*
If you have more than one book write a brief, descriptive paragraph for each. If you have one or two, write longer descriptions.

[2] *ALWAYS put a link to your Amazon page.*
Make sure you don't do a blind link like this: My Book. What if the link doesn't work? People won't know how to reach the page and they're not going to take the time to figure it out. Remember, at this stage everything is an impulse buy. Any obstacle will kill the sale. At the same time, you can't use the whole URL as a link. For example:

http://www.amazon.com/Flirty-Text-Message-Helper-ebook/dp/B0043GX1RQ/ref=sr_1_4?s=digital-text&ie=UTF8&qid=1327414529&sr=1-4

That will junk up your page, make it unreadable, and undesirable. Instead shorten the link by going to www.bit.ly and pasting the Amazon URL into the box. For example, the shortened link to my Flirty Text Message Helper book is...

http://amzn.to/xjUyYj

It's short, not too ugly, and even if the link doesn't work, you can still copy/paste the address into your browser and it will take you directly to my Amazon page.

[3] *Provide contact information.*
This is the place to communicate other products and services if you have them. I strongly suggest you keep this section very short. If you start pitching

like a carnival barker you'll leave people with a bad taste in their mouths. This is also a great opportunity to get feedback on the book, get ideas for the next one or simply get readers signed up to your email list. So many people emailed me with questions and comments that I decided to write an expanded edition for this book even though it's only four months old.

[4] Request a rating and a Facebook share from the Before You Go page.

[5] Request a review and put a link to your book.

Putting It All Together.
To give you a better sense of how all this should flow, let's take a look at how to stage the "gap matter" (information between the end of your book and the appearance of the Before You Go screen):

THE END

Next Page: Author bio.
Next Page: More books from this author.
Next Page: Contact information for feedback and other
                  products and services.
Next Page: A personal request asking readers to rate, share and review.

Depending on the length of your bio and the description of your other books and after-market services, you could conceivably fit everything into two pages, maybe three.

Notes

CHAPTER FIFTEEN

How To Tell How Many Books You Sold By Looking At Your Sales Ranking.

Wouldn't it be great to look at the Amazon sales ranking of a book and know how many it sold? You'd be able to forecast your sales, help select the most profitable categories, and know how much your competitors are making.

I mean, how many books do you sell with an Amazon sales ranking of 50,000? Or 5,000? Or 500?

One thing is for sure--Amazon isn't going to tell you. A well-designed correlation study is the only way to find out. So I kept track of the sales ranking and units sold for six of my ebooks over a 90-day period in 2012. I then commissioned a leading statistician to conduct a correlation study. Could I actually predict how many books I'd sell by simply looking at my Amazon rankings?

The answer is a resounding "Yes, Yes, Oh God, YES!" (my quote, not the statistician's).   The correlation was, in his words, "Magnificent." Now, I am not going to pretend that I understand statistics. The most advanced math book I own is called, Subtraction: Addition's Tricky Friend. So, I am going to let the statistician who conducted my study tell you how it was done (later in this chapter). Now, before we get to the goodies, it will help to understand...

How Amazon Comes Up With Its Sales Ranking.
Let me be clear: No one actually knows the secret sauce to Amazon's logarithms. Still, there are some learned mathematicians and statisticians who've come up with respected theories. I am not one of them. And rather than bloviate about subjects I am not worthy of explaining, I am going to quote extensively from people who do. I asked my statistician to scour the internet for what he thought was the most intelligent, insightful, educated theory of how Amazon's sales ranking works. He pointed me to Morris Rosenthal at http://www.rampant-books.com/mgt_amazon_sales_rank.htm.

Indeed, it is not only a learned analysis but an understandable one. Keep in mind that this analysis is about printed books (though clearly the principles hold for Kindle ebooks):

Amazon's sales rank is calculated as a rolling figure. It's based on sales over a recent period. I can't remember if the period is 60 or 90 days, though. It is, however, weighted by overall total sales (they put this back in after having dropped it for a couple of years), keeping long-term big sellers afloat even after their sharp sales peaks have leveled out.

Not all books are recalculated with the same frequency. The top 1,000 are recalculated hourly. The next block (up to 100,000, I think) are recalculated weekly, while the rest get checked monthly. However, a sudden burst in sales is enough to force an immediate recalculation on a 100,000+ book. This is probably based on a percentage of overall sales, but that's just a guess.

- 1 - 10,000   are recalculated every hour.
- 10,001 - 110,000   are recalculated every day.
- Above 110,001   are recalculated once a month.

To begin with, any book which has no assigned sales rank has yet to sell even one copy on Amazon. So, if you're looking at a book with a sales rank of 4,000,000, then you at least know it has sold at least one copy.

Rosenthal also says that all items are assigned unique rankings. So if you're listed at an Amazon Sales Rank of 34,385 then there are only 34,384 books selling better than yours, and your book is selling better than approximately 4,000,000 other books. Again, for more details, go to http://www.rampant-books.com/mgt_amazon_sales_rank.htm.

How To Tell How Many Books You Sold By Looking At Your Sales Ranking.
Okay, now that you have an understanding of Amazon Sales Ranking (how well your book is doing against all other books), let's lay hands upon the wonderment: The link between sales ranking and books sold. A couple of things you should know going forward:

Most of the numbers you see here are actual, not estimated. Meaning, they're based on my actual sales/rankings, not estimates. The only estimated figures you see will be for sales rankings my books never achieved. For these, my statistician provided estimates as explained below the table.

All sales figures are based on a 24-hour period. This is important to note because depending on how well your book is doing, Amazon updates the rankings hourly. If you don't track figures once daily on a 24-hour basis, you're going to get wild swings that will render your data useless. Here's the process I went through: Every day I would enter my sales ranking and units sold for every book at around 9:00 a.m. This gave me daily, 24-hour totals.

Sales Ranking Within 24 Hour Period	Average # Units Sold	Estimated Or Actual*
1-10	650- 3,000	Estimated
10 – 100	500 - 650	Estimated
100 – 500	200 - 500	Estimated
500 – 1000	150 - 200	Estimated
1,000 – 2,000	70	Actual
2,000 – 3,000	49	Actual
3,000 – 4,000	40	Actual
4,000 - 5,000	24	Actual
5,000 – 6,000	21	Actual
6,000 - 7,000	18	Actual
7,000 – 8,000	15	Actual
8,000 – 9,000	12	Actual
9,000 – 10,000	12	Actual
10,000 – 11,000	11	Actual
11,000 – 12,000	9	Actual
12,000 – 13,000	10	Actual
13,000 – 14,000	9	Actual
14,000 – 15,000	8	Actual
15,000 – 16,000	7	Actual
16,000 – 17,000	6	Actual
17,000 – 18,000	6	Actual
18,000 – 19,000	7	Actual
19,000 – 20,000	5	Actual
20,000 – 21,000	6	Actual
21,000 – 22,000	5	Actual
22,000 – 23,000	5	Actual
23,000 – 24,000	6	Actual
24,000 – 25,000	5	Actual
25,000 – 26,000	5	Actual
26,000 – 27,000	5	Actual
27,000 – 28,000	3	Actual
28,000 – 29,000	4	Actual
29,000 – 30,000	4	Actual
30,000 – 31,000	4	Actual
31,000 – 32,000	3	Actual

32,000 – 33,000	4	Actual
33,000 – 34,000	2	Actual
34,000 – 35,000	2	Actual
35,000 – 36,000	2	Actual
36,000 – 37,000	2	Actual
37,000 – 38,000	2	Actual
38,000 – 39,000	2	Actual
39,000 – 40,000	4	Actual
40,000 – 41,000	2	Actual
41,000 – 42,000	2	Actual
42,000 – 50,000	1.5	Actual
50,000 – 60,000	1.4	Actual
60,000 – 70,000	1.3	Actual
70,000 – 80,000	.8	Actual
80,000 – 90,000	.7	Actual
90,000 – 100,000	.9	Actual
100,000 – 110,000	.4	Actual
110,000 – 120,000	.5	Actual
120,000 – 130,000	.3	Actual
130,000 – 140,000	.2	Actual
140,000 – 150,000	.2	Actual
150,000 – 160,000	.1	Actual
160,000 – 170,000	.1	Actual
170,000 – 500,000	0	Actual

Table Notes

• "Estimated" means I didn't have actual numbers from my own ebooks, so my statistician estimated the figures on the following basis: 1) The trajectory of my own numbers and 2) The statistical analysis done in http://www.rampant-books.com/mgt_amazon_sales_rank.htm, which included an unnamed publisher who released the findings of their study, and statistician Morris Rosenthal's own estimates over at http://www.fonerbooks.com/surfing.htm, which used national probability samples.

• "Actual" means the number of books I sold when I reached a specific sales ranking at the end of a 24-hour period.

• The decimal points reflect the fact that such a high sales ranking produces anywhere between zero and two unit sales, depending on factors known only to Amazon. Obviously, Amazon isn't going to sell .1 of your book. The decimal point is an average over time.

• Kindle books are on a different rating scale from print books.

• Kindle paid and free books are on separate scales.

• Sales correlations are NOT static. Sales ranks only measure relative position, not actual sales, so the corresponding sales will rise and fall in step with Amazon sales in general and also in relation to the size of the Kindle pool of books. The same ranking on different days will produce a different number of sales. A 2,000 ranking on a day that Amazon didn't sell many books is going to produce less sales than the same 2,000 ranking on a day that Amazon does well.

How To Use This Table.
Knowing what Amazon's sales ranking means in terms of units sold has some very useful applications:

1. It will help you project your book's earning potential.
Let's take this book as an example. Before I started writing Make A Killing On Kindle, I wanted to know the size of the market, the leading competitors and how much they were making. But what I really wanted to know was whether writing the book would be worth my time. So here's how I used the table:

    A. <u>I identified my main competitors.</u>
- How I Sold 1 Million eBooks in 5 Months!
- Kindle Cash
- How to Make, Market and Sell Ebooks
- Amazon Kindle Freebies
- Others not worth mentioning

B. I looked at their rankings and used my table to determine their sales.

Book	Sales Ranking Averaged Over A Week's Period	# Of Books Sold Daily	Daily Sales at $4.99 Price	Gross Monthly Sales
How I Sold 1 Million eBooks in 5 Months!	5,000	21	$105	$3,144
Kindle Cash	12,500	10	$50	$1,500
How to Make, Market and Sell Ebooks	13,000	10	$50	$1,500
Amazon Kindle Freebies	14,000	8	$40	$1,198

C. I assessed the strength of my book against my competitors.
It's hard to accurately assess the strength of your book because almost everybody thinks they've written a best seller. That's why most injuries in writing are caused by authors falling off their egos onto their IQs. Don't fall and get hurt--be brutally honest. Does your book have any meaningful advantages over the competition? I felt mine did:

I take a contrarian viewpoint. Every one of my competitors advises that you build a social media platform. I say it's the biggest mistake you could make. I know that a LOT of authors will be drawn to this contrarian message because they've either been using social media (and failing) or have been fearfully contemplating it.

I offer critical information the competition doesn't. For example, how to use HTML code, the relationship between sales ranking and # of units sold, how to get to the top of Amazon's search pages, and how to use its Leading Indicators.

I'm funny. But enough about my looks. My competitors, while capable writers, tend to write on the dry side. I've been writing humor columns for ten years and this gives me a competitive advantage.

D. I used my judgment to project sales.
Looking at the table above, Amazon superstar John Locke leads the pack (his fiction books have sold millions). Given how well known he is I think it's unrealistic to think I could unseat him, even though I believe I have the better book. Fortunately, there is such a pronounced difference in the content of my book and the next two competitors that I find it hard to believe that I won't at least equal their monthly sales. Therefore, I projected

I'd be the second or third best selling book in the category, which would put my gross take around $1,500 a month or $18,000 per year (gross).

UPDATE: It's been three months since the release of my book (and I'm happy to report that my projections were completely wrong. I didn't just beat my #1 competitor; I cleaned his clock. I sell twice as much as Amazon superstar John Locke at nearly twice the price.

Don't take my word for it—check out our Amazon rankings:

John Locke's How I Sold 1 Million eBooks In 5 Months!
Amazon ranking at press time: 4,099.

http://amzn.to/NdRAPY

Make A Killing On Kindle.
Amazon ranking at press time: 2,202.

http://www.amazon.com/dp/B007XVWEIU.

This is fantastic news not just for me, but for you. Because if I, an unknown writer, can use the strategies in this book to unseat a well-known author profiled in The New York Times, so can you.

Let's review. To understand the earnings potential for your book, you should identify your main competitors, look at my table to determine their sales, make an honest assessment of your book's advantages, estimate where you fall in the competitor list (#1? #4? #100?), and project your sales.

Let's continue with other uses for the table...

2. It will help you select the categories for your book.
By knowing the range of sales for the category you're considering, you can avoid categories that don't sell well. Conversely, if the category is a juggernaut, you might want to avoid that, too, since it will be hard to break into. See Chapter Six for a more detailed discussion on how to use the data in this table to assess categories.

3. It will help you figure out what friends, competitors and celebrities are making.
I constantly use this table to figure out what people are making on their books. I simply look at their sales ranking, check it against the table and multiply the number of sales by the price of their book. In less than a minute I can figure out what they're making on a daily and monthly basis. I love calling up my writer friends and saying, "Wow, you sold 20 books today!" It really freaks them out.

How Accurate Is This Table? My Statistician's Comments.
Rather than try to explain why you should trust the accuracy of my table, I'm going to let the statistician who conducted the study do it. For you math wonks, here is the email he sent me:

Mike you are as genius. Your original table was hard to work with. It had three data series: rank, sales, and date. In the new table you aggregated sales and ranks into "bins" for rank meaning ranges such as 6500-7000, and simple averages for sales. As you cleverly deduced, time info is irrelevant. It matters not whether a rank/sales pairing occurs on a Thursday or in January. Why didn't I realize that?

Now, with two variables, it was a piece of cake to run an Excel scatter diagram (below), plotting sales against rank without a time dimension. (I used the midpoint of the high-low range of rank for plotting.) The correlation is magnificent as you can see at a glance. The scatter points show a very high order of correlation, in this case inverse correlation because lower rank correlates with higher sales. If you read the article I sent you the other day you will see that the curve here is very close in shape and slope to the chart the author calculated for a composite of many books.

I then experimented with a curve of best fit, which turned out to be a second-degree polynomial. Don't ask. The curve flattens out at the right side. As rank rises because other books are outgunning you, the correlation becomes more diffuse. This is natural in a series having small numbers at one end, in this case few books.

The mathematical correlation is -0.91, meaning that one variable "explains" 91% of the variation of the other. As I said, the number is negative because low rank goes with high sales. The correlation is extremely high. A common supposition of such is that variation of one of the variables "explains" 91% of the variation of the other. This may seem odd in that many other factors may affect the series, say the economy, competitors to Amazon, and pricing to think of a few. As an example, if you cut the price of your book both sales and ranking would respond favorably. However, the rank and sales may improve at different rates, so the rank/sales correlation might differ significantly from this model, changing the curve and the coefficient of correlation.

Now for the fun part of the analysis. When two series correlate well, usually it is clear which series is the "independent variable" which causes the "dependent variable" to fluctuate. For example, say daily sunshine correlates well with the sunburns that tourists suffer. It's obvious which are the independent and dependent variables. Sunshine causes sunburn, not vice versa. In other instances the correlation is due to a third factor.

As the saying goes, correlation does not imply causation. For example, income and literacy probably correlate well but one does not cause the other. The match is more likely due to other things that drive both series, say education, or culture, or bias.

Your case is fascinating because it's unclear whether sales drive rank (sales as the independent variable) or rank drives sales (rank as the independent variable). Both seem plausible. My guess is that sales are the more likely independent variable. My intuition says it's more likely that sales drive rank even though you have argued plausibly elsewhere that favorable ranks attract more buyers.

BTW, fill in the correct dates in the char title. Do you have Microsoft Excel software?

Notes

CHAPTER SIXTEEN

Tying Everything Into One Glorious Knot.

Feeling overwhelmed? Don't be. There are only twelve action items in this book and they'll only take you about eighteen hours to implement them. I want you to really absorb that. In 18 hours you will have done everything to market your book effectively.

I recommend that you spread those 18 hours over a period of about three weeks. Here's why: Almost every action item in this book requires judgment and creativity. I don't know about you, but my best judgment comes from putting things aside and coming back a few days later to reassess. Whether you're working on keyword phrases or your book title, NEVER make a decision without taking time off to let your creative juices simmer.

You'll also need to budget those eighteen hours over several weeks because some of the work is going to be outsourced (like your book cover) and you're at the mercy of the vendor's timetable. You should also be bouncing ideas off of trusted advisors, which also takes time.

So let's break down the twelve action items and how they amount to 18 hours of work:

1. Designing a book cover: 1 Hour.
Your job is to find and manage the designer. They will do the work. Managing them doesn't take long.

2. Coming up with a clickable title: 4 hours.
Sometimes you get it immediately, other times it will take hours on end. But when you actually add up the hours you spend dreaming up titles, talking to advisors and testing them with your council, it'll be about four hours. It just seems like it takes longer because you're thinking so much about it over the course of a few weeks.

3. Getting to the top of Amazon's search engine: 3 hours.
You'll spend about 2 hours on Google and about 1 hour on Amazon's "Leading Indicators."

4. Picking the categories for your book: .5 hours.
There are only two you can pick. And the way I've laid out the process, it shouldn't take you long at all.

5. Putting a billboard on your competitor's pages: 1 hour.
That includes researching and writing short reviews for three competitive books (with a link to your book).

6. Writing your book description: 3 hours.
It's only 650 words but they better be the best 650 words you've ever written! Treat this with the career-making importance of writing a front-page article for the New York Times. DO NOT PHONE IT IN.

7. Using HTML on your book description: .5 hour.
It really is a copy/paste process, though you will have to test to make sure you didn't screw up.

8. Maximizing your "Look Inside" feature: NA.
Although this will take you some time (2-3 hours), I don't count it as part of the workload because it falls under pre-publication formatting, rather than post-publication marketing. If your book is already published on Kindle and you feel the first 10% of your book's Look Inside feature works against you, I recommend going through the time, energy and expense of re-formatting your book.

9. Pricing strategies: 2 hours.
It's very straightforward: Assess your strengths relative to competitors, look at what they're charging and come up with one of the five launch prices I recommend.

10. Placing strategic starter reviews: 2 hours.
You are essentially writing (or having someone else do it) six insightful reviews. It should take you about 20 minutes per review.

11. Overcoming "Pre-buyers Remorse" with Author Central: .5 hour.
There's simply not much to do on your author page—a short bio and links to your books, blogs and video.

12. Making your book an after-sale ambassador: NA.
Again, this will take you some time but this is a pre-publication formatting issue. If your book is already on Kindle and you don't have an effective post-sales message, it's a judgment call as to whether you should edit, re-format and re-submit. I did it for some of my books, but not for others. However, going forward, I make sure this section is up to snuff before publication.

The 19th Hour & Beyond.
Your job doesn't actually stop after eighteen hours. Once you launch, you have to monitor and manage the process. Things will go wrong. Things that worked suddenly won't. While you should constantly tweak things for the first few months—pricing, categories, book description, etc.—you also have to let things play out. Going forward, keep a couple of things in mind:

Track your sales on a daily basis.
Do it once a day at around the same time in the morning. After a few months (when you're finished with most of the tweaking) you can start tracking it once a week. Tracking reveals trends. And without knowing trends it's easy to panic and make the wrong "repairs." Make sure you stay on top of the tracking.

Know that your sales will hit peaks and valleys.
It's easy to be as nervous as Paris Hilton on Jeopardy when your sales go south. The natural instinct is to panic. Don't. It's natural to have peaks and valleys. I have personally seen my sales shoulder-roll to the floor at 700 MPH only to watch them zoom back up. With no explanation. It's the nature of the beast. Do not be alarmed.

Change one thing at a time.
If your sales are trending downward for two weeks straight, you should definitely take action. But don't make the mistake of changing multiple variables at the same time—that's a great way of obscuring the problem, creating extra work and preventing yourself from understanding the dynamics of your sell trends. If, for example, you think your pricing and book description need a little work, change the price and wait a couple of weeks. If that didn't change the sales trajectory, then change the book description.

Notes

FINAL THOUGHTS.

You have a real shot at making a killing on Kindle. When I first published my ebooks they went on life support. As of this writing, I'm selling about 3,000 books a month. Those sales are strictly a manifestation of the strategies in this book. I don't blog, Facebook, Tweet, send out eblasts, clog editor inboxes with press releases or otherwise, in any way, promote my books.

These strategies work for me, they work for my clients and they'll work for you. I said this earlier but I think it's worth repeating: Believe in your books. Believe in their power to inform, entertain or transform. Believe in your power to put them in the hands of thousands of buyers every month. I never stopped believing in my books. Don't stop believing in yours.

QUESTIONS OR COMMENTS?

I'd love to hear your thoughts. Email me at mike@woodpeckermedia.net.

Need Help?
My company helps authors and publishers turn under-performing books into best sellers. Reach me at mike@woodpeckermedia.net.

Attend My Monthly Webinars!
See live demonstrations of the concepts in this book, get your questions answered in real time and set your book on the path to profits. Sign up at *www.howtosellonkindle.net/webinars*.

One Last Thing...
When you turn the page, Kindle will give you the opportunity to rate the book and share your thoughts through an automatic feed to your Facebook and Twitter accounts. If you believe your friends would get something valuable out of this book, I'd be honored if you'd post your thoughts.

If you feel particularly strong about the contributions this book made to your own marketing efforts, I'd be eternally grateful if you posted a review on Amazon. Just click here and it will take you directly to the page: http://amzn.to/N52RSC.

All the best,

Michael